DOMINION AND
COMMON GRACE

Other books by Gary North

Marx's Religion of Revolution, 1968
An Introduction to Christian Economics, 1973
Unconditional Surrender, 1981
Successful Investing in an Age of Envy, 1981
The Dominion Covenant: Genesis, 1982
Government by Emergency, 1983
The Last Train Out, 1983
Backward, Christian Soldiers?, 1984
75 Bible Questions Your Instructors
    Pray You Won't Ask, 1984
Coined Freedom: Gold in the Age of
    the Bureaucrats, 1984
Moses and Pharaoh, 1985
Negatrends, 1985
The Sinai Strategy, 1986
Unholy Spirits: Occultism and
    New Age Humanism, 1986
Conspiracy: A Biblical View, 1986
Inherit the Earth, 1987
Honest Money, 1986
Fighting Chance, 1986 [with Arthur Robinson]
Resurrection vs. Entropy, 1987
The Pirate Economy, 1987
Liberating Planet Earth, 1987
    (Spanish) *Teología de Liberación*, 1986

Books edited by Gary North

Foundations of Christian Scholarship, 1976
Tactics of Christian Resistance, 1983
The Theology of Christian Resistance, 1983
Editor, *Journal of Christian Reconstruction* (1974-1981)

DOMINION AND COMMON GRACE

The Biblical Basis of Progress

Gary North

Institute for Christian Economics
Tyler, Texas

Published in Tyler, Texas
by Institute for Christian Economics

Distributed by Dominion Press
7112 Burns Street, Fort Worth, Texas 76118

Printed in the United States of America

ISBN 0-930464-09-5

This book is dedicated to

John Frame

an uncommonly gracious man,
who will no doubt conclude that
portions of this book are good,
other portions are questionable,
but the topic warrants further study.

TABLE OF CONTENTS

PREFACE

And when the thousand years are expired, Satan shall be loosed out of his prison, and shall go out to deceive the nations which are in the four quarters of the earth, Gog and Magog, to gather them together to battle: the number of whom is as the sand of the sea. And they went up on the breadth of the earth, and compassed the camp of the saints about, and the beloved city: and fire came down from God out of heaven, and devoured them (Rev. 20:8-9).

As you probably know, Christians disagree about the doctrine of "the last things," called *eschatology* ["eskaTOLogy"]. I firmly believe that conservative Protestants in the United States are about to get into the biggest theological shouting match of this century over the question of eschatology.

But there is one point that 99.9% of all Bible-believing Christians agree on: these verses in the Book of Revelation refer to the events immediately preceding the final judgment. No denomination or

school of theological interpretation within the orthodox Christian camp argues against this.

This identification of these verses with the final
judgment raises a key question of interpretation that
non-postmillennialists repeatedly ask postmillennialists (whenever they can locate one). It is a reasonable
question:

> "How does the postmillennialist explain the
> final rebellion of Satan at the end of history?"

There may be a few isolated postmillennialists
who deny that this prophecy refers to a rebellion at
the end of history, but such a view makes little im
pression on anyone who reads Revelation 20. Those
who accept the plain teaching of Revelation 20 must
admit that a rebellion occurs at the very end of history. In fact, this rebellion calls down God's fire from
heaven which ends history.

Is the whole world going to be deceived, except
for a handful of Christians? The language of Revelation 20:8 is not clear enough to conclude for certain
that the devil actually succeeds in deceiving all the
nations of the earth, whose inhabitants number as
the sands of the sea. He will go out to do so, but he
may not be completely successful. But it is possible
that Satan will successfully deceive a majority of
those who will be living at that time.

It should also be clear that the deception is a
deception of *people*. The battle between God and
Satan is for the souls of men. Revelation 20:8-9 is
not talking primarily about angels. It is also not

describing a contest over power. There is no question about who has more power in history: God does. What this describes is a battle primarily over *ethics*. "Choose this day whom you will serve," Elijah demanded of the people of Israel (I Kings 18). This is *the* question of life for every man and society in history. The answer that men give has life-and-death consequences, as it had for the 850 false prophets whom Elijah ordered the people to grab, and whom he then killed (18:40), just as they would have killed him had God's fire not burned up the sacrifice on the altar Elijah built. But the fire came down to consume the right sacrifice, and judgment then came to the false prophets. So it will be again at that last day, only next time the fire will consume the false prophets directly, overcoming and ending human judgments in history.

Satan's lure has been the same from the days of the garden of Eden: to get men to covenant with him rather than God, to place themselves under his jurisdiction rather than God's jurisdiction. And let us not forget, "jurisdiction" comes from two Latin words that mean "law" (*juris*) and "saying" (*diction-em*). When Satan and God speak their rival laws, whose law will men obey? It is a battle between sovereigns and their respective laws. It is a battle for the hearts, minds, and souls of men. It is also a battle for their *strength* (Luke 10:27). To that extent, it is a struggle for power, but only because biblical ethics is the source of all long-term power.[1] This, too, is a central theme of this book.

---

1. Gary North, *Moses and Pharaoh: Dominion Religion vs. Power Religion* (Tyler, Texas: Institute for Christian Economics, 1985).

The Battlefield

A war will be fought at that last day — a very brief war. Where will it be fought? What exactly will be the battlefield? What do the words mean, "compassed the camp of the saints about, and the beloved city"? Are there two literal places in view, the camp of the saints *and* the beloved city? Is this one place, with two descriptions? Or are the words symbolic of Christians in general and the church in general?

I know of no commentator who accepts literally the idea that the entire population of Christian believers is holed up in one city, even "the beloved city." There may be such an interpreter, but I have not come across him. Perhaps some dispensationalist interpreter somewhere does cling to such literalism. In response, I would ask him two questions, using basic dispensationalist teaching concerning the millennium: "First, where on earth are the millions upon millions of previously Raptured, transformed, now-immortal believers who returned to earth with Jesus, and who have been living all over the earth for the past one thousand years? Second, are all the Christians on earth — Raptured saints and post-Rapture converts — living in Jerusalem?" I think these questions dispose of the literal city view. The battlefield will be larger than Jerusalem.

Conventional premillennial interpreters might argue that the second reference could be to Jerusalem, but that not every believer on earth is there. It is simply a representative city. The same satanic attack will be going on elsewhere. The "camp of the saints" is the whole earth. This would make more sense.

Those who are not premillennialists usually argue that "the camp of the saints" and "the beloved city" both refer symbolically to the church, and probably the invisible church, meaning the totality of individual Christians. An attack by Satan's human followers comes on those who are true Christians.

One question for all interpreters arises: How will the satanists know who is who? Christians cannot be sure about the true spiritual status of members of our own congregations at any point in time. This is why God requires excommunications to deal with church members who commit major sins. How will Satan's human army identify clearly just who the true Christians are? Or will the attack be somewhat indiscriminate? This problem besets all interpreters.

However large the army of Satan may be, Revelation 20 indicates that there will be a sufficient number of reprobates to surround the Christians, meaning sufficient to threaten them with death. This will be a confrontation primarily between rival armies of mortals, not between armies of angels or between anyone and Raptured immortals (in the premillennial scheme) who obviously cannot be threatened with death. (The premillennialist really does have a problem in explaining where all those Raptured immortals will be when the war breaks out, and what they will be doing to defend their mortal Christian brothers.) This is clearly a description of a huge, well-organized army of evil people.

The attack is unsuccessful. Immediately, God intervenes, burns them up, and begins the last judg-

ment. The resurrection of the dead takes place. End
of history. Curtain call. Boos and cheers from the
heavenly host.

The Postmillennialist's Problem

The postmillennialist argues that the kingdom of
God is to be progressively manifested on earth before the day of judgment, and therefore before the
Rapture, which he identifies with the last judgment.
Then how can these events take place? Where will
all those sinners come from? The army of Satan will
be filled with people who have been recruited from
the nations of the earth, not angels.

We need to consider several possible assumptions
that may be coloring the exegesis of either postmillennialists or the questioners.

1. Does a theology of the extension of
God's kingdom on earth require that almost
everyone on earth in the era close to that final
day be a born-again believer in Christ?

2. Can born-again believers fall from grace
and then rebel? In short, can Satan gain recruits from the born-again invisible church?

3. Can unbelievers seem to be saints in the
camp of the saints, almost as spies who successfully invade an enemy military camp?

4. How can unbelievers possess so much
power after generations of Christian dominion?

The answer to the first two questions is "no."
Postmillennialism does not require that all or even

most people be converts to Christ at that last day.
(Prior to the last day, postmillennialism holds, there
will be large numbers of converts, and the civilization of the world will generally reflect God's biblically revealed law-order.) People at that last day
need only be externally obedient to the terms of the
covenant, meaning biblical law. This book attempts
to explain how this externally faithful living might
operate.

The question of whether saints can fall from
grace is not a specifically eschatological issue, but I
know of no postmillennial commentator who believes that men can fall from special (soul-saving)
grace. Obviously, if regenerate men can lose their
salvation, then there is no big problem for the postmillennialist in explaining the final rebellion at the
last day. This book is dealing with a harder problem.

The answer to the third question is "yes." The
camp of the saints can and will be filled with people
who have the outward signs of faith but not the in-
ward marks. In fact, this is the only way out of the
exegetical dilemma for the postmillennialist.

If the answer to question number one is "no, not
everyone needs to be a saint," then this raises a fifth
question:

"How can a world full of reprobates be considered a manifestation of the kingdom of God
on earth?"

The answers to the fourth and fifth questions are
closely related to each other. Answering these two

questions is what this book is all about. The correct answers come when we gain a correct understanding of the much-neglected doctrine of common grace.

The reader should understand in advance that this book is not intended to present the exegetical case for postmillennialism. I no more try to build the case for postmillennialism here than Van Til tries to build the case for amillennialism in *Common Grace and the Gospel*. I simply assume it, and then get on with the business at hand. This is an exercise in apologetics, not systematics. David Chilton's *Paradise Restored* and *Days of Vengeance* have presented the case for postmillennialism better than I could or any other theologian ever has. Any critic who thinks that he will score cosmic Brownie points by saying, "But North doesn't *prove* his eschatology" should get on with *his* business at hand, namely, writing a definitive critique of Chilton's eschatology books. That project will keep him busy for a few years. (Furthermore, unless he is very, very bright, and very, very gifted stylistically, it will also end his career as a critic when he finally gets it into print, *if* he can get it into print.)

INTRODUCTION

*Another parable put he forth unto them, saying,
The kingdom of heaven is likened unto a man which
sowed good seed in his field. But while men slept, his
enemy came and sowed tares among the wheat, and
went his way. But when the blade was sprung up, and
brought forth fruit, then appeared the tares also. So the
servants of the householder came and said unto him,
Sir, didst thou not sow good seed in thy field? From
whence then hath it tares? He said unto them, An
enemy hath done this. The servants said unto him,
Wilt thou then that we go and gather them up? But he
said, Nay; lest while ye gather up the tares, ye root up
also the wheat with them. Let both grow together until
the harvest: and in the time of harvest I will say to the
reapers, Gather ye together first the tares, and bind
them in bundles to burn them: but gather the wheat into
my barn (Matt. 13:24-30).*

This passage deals with the kingdom of God. It
raises one of the most important issues in human

thought, the issue of "continuity vs. discontinuity."

The discontinuity in this passage is the final judgment. Will the owner of the field (God) allow the servants (angels) to tear out the tares (evil men) before the harvest date (the end of time)? The answer is *no*. The owner insists that the tares be left alone until both wheat and tares have fully matured, and the harvest day has come.

God's plan for history involves both continuity and discontinuity. His continuity is His grace. "The Lord is gracious, and full of compassion; slow to anger, and of great mercy" (Ps. 145:8). The phrase *slow to anger* is crucial. Eventually, He brings judgment, but only after time passes. But judgment eventually comes to the wicked: "The Lord preserveth all them that love him: but all the wicked will he destroy" (Ps. 145:20). God announced the following to Moses, after Moses had completed his task of carving the ten commandments into two stones:

And the Lord passed by before him, and proclaimed, The Lord God, merciful and gracious, longsuffering, and abundant in goodness and truth, keeping mercy for thousands, forgiving iniquity and transgression and sin, and that will by no means clear the guilty; visiting the iniquity of the fathers upon the children, and upon the children's children, unto the third and to the fourth generation (Ex. 34:5-7).

The Lord suffers long; in this case, three or four generations. This is exactly what God had told

Abraham concerning the conquest of the Promised Land: "But in the fourth generation they shall come hither again: for the iniquity of the Amorites is not yet full" (Gen. 15:16). In the fourth generation after they became subservient to Egypt, the Israelites would return. Moses' generation was the fourth after Jacob came down to Egypt (Levi, Kohath, Amram, Moses: Ex. 6:16, 18, 20). They came to the edge of the land, but drew back in fear; Joshua's generation conquered it.

Why the delay in judging the Amorites? Their iniquity was not yet full. God gave them time to fill it up. He gave them *continuity.* Then, in Joshua's day, he gave them discontinuity. Judgment came at last.

So it is with the history of man. God extends time to all men; then, at the final day (or at the death of each person), judgment comes. Judgment day confirms eternal life to the regenerate, and the second death (Rev. 20:14) to the unregenerate. Continuity is broken by discontinuity.

Common Grace

If you want a four-word summary of this book, here it is: *common grace is continuity.* It is also a prelude to judgment.

The concept of common grace is seldom discussed outside of Calvinistic circles, although all Christian theologies must eventually come to grips with the issues underlying the debate over common grace. The phrase was employed by colonial American Puritans. I came across it on several occasions when I was doing research on the colonial Puritans' economic doctrines and economic experiments. The concept goes back at least to John Calvin's writings.[1]

Before venturing into the forest of theological debate, let me state what I believe is the meaning of the word "grace." The Bible uses the idea in several ways, but the central meaning of grace is this: a gift given to God's creatures on the basis, first, of His favor to His Son, Jesus Christ, the incarnation of the second person of the Trinity, and second, on the basis of Christ's atoning work on the cross. Grace is not strictly unmerited, for Christ merits every gift, but in terms of the merit of the creation — merit deserved by a creature because of its mere creaturehood — there is none. In short, when we speak of any aspect of the creation, other than the incarnate Jesus Christ, grace is defined as an *unmerited gift*. The essence of grace is conveyed in James 1:17: "Every good gift and every perfect gift is from above, and cometh down from the Father of lights, with whom is no variableness, neither shadow of turning."

Special grace is the phrase used by theologians to describe the gift of eternal salvation. Paul writes: "For by grace are ye saved through faith; and that not of yourselves: it is the gift of God: Not of works, lest any man should boast" (Eph. 2:8-9). He also writes: "But God commendeth his love toward us, in that, while we were yet sinners, Christ died for us" (Rom. 5:8). God selects those on whom He will have mercy (Rom. 9:18). He has chosen these people to be

---

1. John Calvin, *Institutes of the Christian Religion* (1559), Book II, Chapter II, sections 13-17; II:III:3; III:XIV:2.

recipients of His gift of eternal salvation, and He chose them before the foundation of the world (Eph. 1:4-6).

But there is another kind of grace, and it is misunderstood. *Common grace* is equally a gift of God to His creatures, but it is distinguished from special grace in a number of crucial ways. The key verse that describes two kinds of grace is I Timothy 4:10: "For therefore we both labour and suffer reproach, because we trust in the living God, who is the Saviour of all men, specially of those that believe." This verse unquestionably states that *Jesus Christ is the Savior of all men, meaning all people.* Yet the Bible does not teach "universalism," meaning the ethical redemption of all men. There are saved and lost throughout eternity (Rev. 20:14). So what does this verse mean? It means simply that Christ died for all men, giving unmerited gifts to all men *in time and on earth.* Some people go to eternal destruction, and others are resurrected to live with Christ eternally. But all men have at least the unmerited gift of life, at least for a time. There are therefore two kinds of salvation: special (eternal) and temporal (earthly).

A debate has gone on for close to a century within Calvinistic circles concerning the nature and reality of common grace. I hope that this little book will contribute some acceptable answers to the people of God, though I have little hope of convincing those who have been involved in this debate for 60 years.

Because of the confusion associated with the term "common grace," let me offer James Jordan's description of it. Common grace is the equivalent of the crumbs that fall from the master's table that the dogs eat. This is how the Canaanite woman described her request of healing by Jesus, and Jesus healed her daughter because of her understanding and faith (Matt. 15:27-28).[2] The prime loaf, however, is reserved for those who respond in faith to the gospel, and who then persevere in this faith to the end of their earthly lives (Matt. 13:8, 23).

Background of the Debate

In 1924, the Christian Reformed Church debated the subject of common grace, and the decision of the Synod led to a major division within the ranks of the denomination which has yet to be healed. The debate was of considerable interest to Dutch Calvinists on both sides of the Atlantic, although traditional American Calvinists were hardly aware of the issue, and Arminian churches were (and are still) completely unaware of it. Herman Hoeksema, who was perhaps the most brilliant systematic theologian in America in this century, left the Christian Reformed Church to form the Protestant Reformed Church. He and his followers were convinced that, contrary to the decision of the CRC, there is no such thing as common grace.

The doctrine of common grace, as formulated in

---

2. Dogs in Israel were not highly loved animals, so the analogy with common grace is biblically legitimate. "And ye shall be holy men unto me: neither shall ye eat any flesh that is torn of beasts in the field; ye shall cast it to the dogs" (Ex. 22:31). If we assume that God loves pagans the way that modern people love their dogs, then the analogy will not fit.

the disputed "three points" of the Christian Reformed Church in 1924, asserts the following:

1. Concerning *the favorable attitude of God toward mankind in general and not only toward the elect*, the Synod declares that according to Scripture and the Confession it is certain that, besides the saving grace of God bestowed only upon those chosen to eternal life, there is also a certain favor or grace of God manifested to His creatures in general. . . .[3]

2. Concerning *the restraint of sin in the life of the individual and of society*, the Synod declares that according to Scripture and the Confession there is such a restraint of sin. . . .[4]

3. Concerning *the performance of so-called civic righteousness by the unregenerate*, the Synod declares that according to Scripture and the Confession the unregenerate, although incapable of any saving good (*Canons of Dort*, III, IV:3), can perform such civic good. . . .[5]

These principles can serve as a starting point for a discussion of common grace.

3. R. B. Kuiper, *To Be or Not to Be Reformed: Whither the Christian Reformed Church?* (Grand Rapids, Michigan: Zondervan, 1959), p. 105. Van Til's version was taken from *The Banner* (June 1, 1939), and differs slightly in the wording. I have decided to use Kuiper's summary. Van Til, *Common Grace*, in *Common Grace and the Gospel* (Nutley, New Jersey: Presbyterian & Reformed, 1972), pp. 19-20.
4. *Idem.*
5. *Ibid.*, pp. 105-6.

The serious Christian eventually will be faced with the problem of explaining the good once he faces the biblical doctrine of evil. James 1:17 informs us that all good gifts are from God. The same point is made in Deuteronomy 8:18. It is clear that the unregenerate are the beneficiaries of God's gifts. None of the participants to the debate denies the existence of the gifts. What is denied by the Protestant Reformed critics is that these gifts imply the *favor of God* as far as the unregenerate are concerned. They categorically deny the first point of the original three points.

For the moment, let us refrain from using the word grace. Instead, let us limit ourselves to the word *gift*. The existence of gifts from God raises a whole series of questions:

Does a gift from God imply His favor?

Does an unregenerate man possess the power to do good?

Does the existence of good behavior on the part of the unbeliever deny the doctrine of total depravity?

Does history reveal a progressive separation between saved and lost?

Would such a separation necessarily lead to the triumph of the unregenerate?

Is there a common ground intellectually between Christians and non-Christians?

Can Christians and non-Christians cooperate successfully in certain areas?

Do God's gifts increase or decrease over time?

Will the cultural mandate (dominion covenant) of Genesis 1:28 be fulfilled?

This little book is my attempt to provide preliminary answers to these questions.

Challenging Van Til

This book is basically a refutation of Prof. Cornelius Van Til's book, *Common Grace and the Gospel*, a compilation of his essays on common grace. It is without question the worst book he ever wrote. It is also one of the most confusing books he ever wrote, given the relative simplicity of the topic. It was not as though he was trying to analyze and refute the arcane mental meanderings of some dead German theologian. It is possible to write a clear book on common grace.

It is not that Van Til's book is not filled with many important insights into many philosophical and theological problems. The trouble is, these insights are found in any of a dozen other of his books. The vast bulk of these insights really did not belong in *Common Grace and the Gospel*. If he had removed them, he would have spared us all a lot of time and trouble, not to mention a lot of extra paper—and it possibly would have spared us several of his mistakes. But probably not. Van Til has referred to himself as a stubborn Dutchman.[6] He clings to his

---

6. William White, Jr., *Van Til: Defender of the Faith* (Nashville, Tennessee: Thomas Nelson, 1979), p. 89.

favorite mistakes with the same fervency that he clings to his favorite truths.

This raises a much-neglected point. Van Til is an enigma to those of us who studied under him or who have struggled through his books. His books are always filled with brilliant insights, but it is very difficult to remember where any single insight appeared. They are scattered like loose diamonds throughout his writings, but they never seem to fit in any particular slot. Any given insight might just as well be in any of his books—or all of them. (In fact, it may be in all of them.) They are not systematically placed brilliant insights. They are just brilliant. He makes good use from them, too; he repeats the same ones in many of his books. "No use throwing this away after only one time; it's almost like new. I'll use it again!" The man is clearly Dutch.

His most effective critical arguments sound the same in every book. Randomly pick up a coverless Van Til book, and start reading; you may not be sure from the development of the arguments just what the book is about, or who it is intended to refute. His books all wind up talking about the same three dozen themes. (Or is it four dozen?) Just keep reading. You will probably find his favorite Greeks: Plato, who struggled unsuccessfully to reconcile Parmenides and Heraclitus. But only rarely will you find a footnote to one of their primary source documents.[7]

---

7. The remarkable thing is that Van Til knows his primary source material better than most philosophers. As a graduate student at Princeton University, he studied under the famous and rigorous classical scholar-philosopher, A. A. Bowman. He

Kant's name will be there, too, but only in a four-page string of quotations from a book written in 1916 or 1932 by a scholar you have never heard of. (No direct citations from Kant? Hardly ever. Phenomenal!) He will refer to a Bible verse occasionally, but the rarest diamond of all is a page of detailed Bible exposition.[8] You will learn about univocal and equivocal reasoning. Continuity will be challenging discontinuity. Rationalism will be doing endless battle with irrationalism. The one will be smothering the many, whenever the many aren't overwhelming the one. (These last four conflicts are, if I understand him correctly, all variations of essentially the same intellectual problem.)

Watch for his analogies. Rationalism and irrationalism will be taking in each other's washing for a living. There will be a chain of being lying around somewhere, probably right next to the infinitely long cord that the beads with no holes are supposed to decorate. Some child will be trying to slap her father's face while sitting on his lap, and someone out in the garage will be sharpening a buzz saw that is set at the wrong angle. Warning: if you don't watch your step, you could trip over the full-bucket problem. And so it goes, book after book.

---

and his two fellow students (including another of my teachers, Philip Wheelwright) would be assigned a passage in Plato or Aristotle in the original Greek. They would then go into the seminar to discuss what they had read.

8. An exception is the first half of *The God of Hope* (Phillipsburg, New Jersey: Presbyterian & Reformed, 1978). These chapters are sermons. But there is not much exegesis even here.

What memorable analogies! But where did I read the one about the ladder of water rising out of the water to the water above? Which bad argument of which philosopher did that one wash away?

What we need is a 5-inch laser disk hooked to a Sony . . . scratch that . . . a Philips (Dutch) laser disk player with a microchip, with all of his works on the disk, plus a computer program that will search every phrase and pull the one we want onto the screen in three seconds. The technology exists; the market for his works doesn't. Sad.

Puzzling

F. A. Hayek says that great scholarly minds come in two types. There are system-builders whose minds encompass huge amounts of seemingly disparate information and then pull them into a coherent whole. There are also those who Hayek calls puzzlers. These men take the great systems, break them into scattered sections, and start pointing out the problems with every single part, often from a perspective that few people have thought of and fewer yet can follow.[9]

Van Til is a classic puzzler. In (non-brute) fact, he built his epistemology quite frankly in terms of his view that all man's attempts to build totally comprehensive systems are doomed to failure, that all human thought is the exercise of puzzling. God is in-

---

9. F. A. Hayek, "Two Types of Mind," *Encounter* (Sept. 1975); reprinted in Hayek, *New Studies in Philosophy, Politics, Economics and the History of Ideas* (Chicago: University of Chicago Press, 1978), ch. 4.

finite; man is finite. Man's mind will never comprehend (surround, encircle) God. Man's mind will therefore never encompass any aspect of the creation, for every atom is related to God, and this brings God back into the picture. The atom, too, is incomprehensible by man's finite mind. But God comprehends Himself and His creation, so we must go to God's Word to begin locating the proper ways to puzzle through any problem. As the person who keeps turning a blade of grass over and over, getting more knowledge of it each time, but never seeing both sides at once, so is man's ability to observe and think.

Van Til takes any system you hand him, and he breaks it down into its component parts, turning the pieces over and over in his mind, finding out what it is and how it works. The problem is, he never puts the pieces back together. He just leaves them scattered around on the floor. "Next!"

On the floor, in pieces, they all look pretty much alike. Go ahead. Pick up that scrap of Barthianism. The one over there. No, no—the *other* one. (*Wholly other.*) Doesn't it resemble a fragment from Kant? Or is it more like Heraclitus? Or could it really be a direct descendent of Plato?

One thing you will recognize for sure: it's humanism.[10]

The Wrong Questions

Van Til has only a finite number of questions to ask about each system, and some are his special

---

10. Van Til, *Christianity and Barthianism* (Philadelphia: Presbyterian & Reformed, 1962).

favorites. These are the ones he usually asks. Of course, he has lots more in reserve. The trouble is, he sometimes asks less appropriate questions, just because he likes his favorites so much. *Common Grace and the Gospel* suffers from this flaw. Other questions should have been asked, but he is determined to ask the questions he wants to ask, and others just will not do. Even better ones.

In this book, I try to ask better questions.

Why attack Van Til? Because he is the best. If some theological nonentity had written *Common Grace and the Gospel*, it would not matter if anyone replied to him. But it matters with Van Til. He is the man who has reconstructed Christian philosophy in our time, by far the most important Christian philosopher of all time. His dissecting and puzzling have cut apart all the alternative systems. He has knocked all the Humpty Dumpties off their respective walls. But when he goes in to try to put a case of biblical eggs in their place, he sometimes slips in the goo.

He simply slipped up (or fell down) with *Common Grace and the Gospel*.

So, what is wrong with his book on common grace? First, it is cluttered up with extraneous material. The book is filled with questions concerning Platonic reasoning, Roman Catholic apologetics, and other specialized philosophical topics. But these topics are not the heart of the debate over common grace. As with everything else Van Til writes about, he can use them to illustrate philosophical topics, but in this case, this overemphasis on philosophy misleads the reader. It steers him away from the key issue. This is my second (and major) criticism.

What the common grace debate is about, above all, is *history*. The issue of common grace asks: What is the history of the saved and the lost in God's scheme of things? Where are men headed, and why? We find the answer right where Van Til always says we must search for every philosophical answer: in ethics.

In short, common grace is about *eschatology*. And it is here that Van Til's stubborn Dutchmanship is rock-hard. He will not budge. He is an amillennialist. Worse: he is an *undeclared* amillennialist. He builds his whole theory of common grace in terms of his hidden eschatology, probably never realizing the extent to which his seemingly philosophical exposition is in fact structured by his assumptions concerning eschatology.

So forget about Plato. Forget about St. Thomas Aquinas. Forget about univocal vs. equivocal reasoning. Keep your eye on his prophetic chart. If it is wrong, then the whole book is wrong.

And just to get my position straight right from the beginning, let me say this: his prophecy chart is wrong.

The righteousness of the perfect shall direct his way: but the wicked shall fall by his own wickedness.

The righteousness of the upright shall deliver them: but transgressors shall be taken in *their own* naughtiness.

When a wicked man dieth, *his* expectation shall perish: and the hope of unjust *men* perisheth.

The righteous is delivered out of trouble, and the wicked cometh in his stead.

Prov. 11:5-8

1

THE FAVOR OF GOD

> *Do not I hate them, O LORD, that hate thee? And
> am I not grieved with those that rise up against thee? I
> hate them with a perfect hatred: I count them mine ene-
> mies (Ps. 139:21-22).*

> *For the scripture saith unto Pharaoh, Even for this
> same purpose have I raised thee up, that I might shew
> my power in thee, and that my name might be declared
> throughout all the earth. Therefore hath he mercy on
> whom he will have mercy, and whom he will he hard-
> eneth (Rom. 9:17-18).*

"Perfect love casteth out fear" (I John 4:18). If
David's encounter with Goliath is evidence, so does
perfect hatred against God's enemies. David was the
greatest warrior in Israel's history; I would argue
that this was to a large degree because he hated
God's enemies with a perfect hatred. The perfect
love of God necessarily involves the perfect hatred of
God's enemies.

Van Til has argued that men are to think God's

thoughts after Him. Men think analogically and re-creatively. We think as creatures, not creators. David the psalmist thought analogically to God. He hated God's enemies with a perfect hatred. His perfect hatred of God's enemies as a sinful and limited man points to God's perfect hatred as a perfect and omnipotent God. God's perfect hatred makes Him a warrior, too. What is an enemy army in the face of such a warrior? This should remind us, "What shall we then say to these things? If God be for us, who can be against us?" (Rom. 8:31). God, the perfect hater, will break all His opposition. His church will march in victory behind this perfect warrior. God hates His enemies without compromise or shadow of turning. As history progresses, God's holy hatred will become increasingly operational and increasingly visible, until that final day when His perfect hatred will become institutionalized in the lake of fire (Rev. 20:14). History should be understood as the working out of God's implacable hatred of His enemies, human and demonic, alongside of His irresistible grace and mercy to God's people. The hatred of God and the love of God are equally ultimate in principle, and this equal ultimacy will become visible as history progresses.

This leads us to what unfortunately became the key question in the twentieth-century debate over common grace: "Does God in any way favor the covenant-breaker?" This has been the focus of the argument in the last 60 years between those who affirm and those who deny the existence of common grace. This was the debate that split the Christian Reformed Church in 1924, and an endless recounting of that debate by the splinter church, the Protestant Reformed Church, keeps that church's distinctives alive. (The Christian Reformed Church is now debating the ordination of women elders, so the theological and epistemological subtleties of the debate over common grace have long since eluded them.)

I argue in this book that the narrow focus of this debate muddied the waters. The key issues of the common grace debate are eschatological and covenantal, not meteorological (see the next subsection: Matt. 5:44-45). Nevertheless, I wish to save time, though not trouble, so let me say from the outset that the Christian Reformed Church's 1924 formulation of the first point is defective. The Bible does not indicate that God in any way favors the unregenerate. It says the opposite. "He that believeth on the Son hath everlasting life: and he that believeth not the Son shall not see life; but the wrath of God abideth on him" (John 3:36). The wrath of God abides on the unbeliever in the present. But as we shall see, this wrath takes the form of *favors* (not favor) shown to the unbeliever in history.

Ethical Separation, Common Gifts
There is a fundamental ethical separation between the saved and the lost. God hated Esau and loved Jacob, before either was born (Rom. 9:10-13). The ninth chapter of Romans and these verses in particular may bother some people, but they shouldn't. The startling fact described here is not that God hated Esau before he was born, for Esau,

like all men, was a son of Adam. The sons of Adam automatically come under the covenantal curse of God against Adam. Sin, after all, is *original* sin. The startling fact is that God loved Jacob before he was born. Sin-influenced men, unfortunately, tend to be startled by the fact that God hated "innocent" unborn Esau, as if men were in any sense innocent before God in their fallen condition at any point in their lives. People are legally innocent at birth before the courts of men, which is why abortion is murder, but they are never innocent in the perfect court of God. They do not need to reach a supposed "age of discretion" in order to be condemned by God. Esau didn't need to be born to come under God's wrath, nor did Jacob need to be born to come under God's favor. Adam's sin doomed Esau, while Christ's atoning work saved Jacob. God imputed Adam's sin to Esau, and Christ's atonement to Jacob, according to the perfect counsel of His sovereign will. As Paul wrote concerning the mercy of God, "Therefore hath he mercy on whom he will have mercy, and whom he will he hardeneth" (Rom. 9:18).

If this bothers you in any way, let me issue a warning: you are thinking humanistically.

God's Gifts to the Unregenerate

What are we to make of the Bible's passages that have been used to support the idea of limited favor toward creatures (including demons) in general? Without exception, they refer to *gifts* of God to the unregenerate. They do not imply God's favor.

The 1924 Synod stated categorically and without

THE FAVOR OF GOD

qualification, "Concerning the favorable attitude of God toward mankind in general and not only toward the elect, the Synod declares that according to Scripture and the Confession it is certain that, besides the saving grace of God bestowed only upon those chosen to eternal life, there is also a certain favor or grace of God manifested to His creatures in general. . . ."[1] I assume that *creatures in general* means, basically, creatures in general. If the Synod had wanted to exclude Satan and his demonic host, it had that opportunity in 1924, when its actions led to the splitting of the church and the exodus of a large portion of its more theologically conservative members. The fact that it refused to exclude Satan has created some real problems for Van Til, and it has placed in the hands of the Protestant Reformed Church a large-caliber theological gun.

I argue throughout this book that there can be no favor shown to "creatures in general," since "creatures in general" includes Satan. The historical and eternal problem facing Satan is that his status as an angel no longer protects him from God's wrath and perfect hatred; he is in sin, which makes him a fallen angel. Similarly, the historical and eternal problem facing ethical rebels is that their status as men made in God's image no longer protects them from God's wrath and perfect hatred; they are in sin, which makes them reprobates. God therefore shows no favor to them, any more than He shows favor to

---

1. R. B. Kuiper, *To Be or Not to Be Reformed: Whither the Christian Reformed Church?* (Grand Rapids, Michigan: Zondervan, 1959), p. 105.

Satan. But He does shower them with non-favorable favors, just as He showers Satan with them.

What are some biblical examples of these non-favorable favors? There is this affirmation: "The Lord is good to all: and his tender mercies are over all his works" (Ps. 145:9). The verse preceding this one tells us that God is compassionate, slow to anger, and gracious. Romans 2:4 tells us He is long-suffering. Luke 6:35-36 says:

> But love ye your enemies, and do good, and lend, hoping for nothing again; and your reward shall be great, and ye shall be the children of the Highest: for he is kind unto the unthankful and to the evil. Be ye therefore merciful, as your Father also is merciful.

First Timothy 4:10, cited in the introduction, uses explicit language: "For therefore we both labour and suffer reproach, because we trust in the living God, who is the Saviour of all men, specially of those that believe." The Greek word here translated as "Saviour" is transliterated *soter*: one who saves, heals, protects, or makes whole. God saves (heals) everyone, *especially* those who believe. Unquestionably, the salvation spoken of is universal—not in the sense of special grace, so therefore in the sense of common grace. This is probably the most difficult verse in the Bible for those who deny universal salvation from hell, yet who also deny the existence of common grace.[2]

---

2. Gary North, "Aren't There Two Kinds of Salvation?", Question 75 in North, *75 Bible Questions Your Instructors Pray You Won't Ask* (Tyler, Texas: Spurgeon Press, 1984).

The most frequently cited passage used by those who defend the idea of God's favor to the unregenerate is Matthew 5:44-45:

But I say unto you, Love your enemies, bless them that curse you, do good to them that hate you, and pray for them which despitefully use you, and persecute you; That ye may be the children of your Father which is in heaven: for he maketh his sun to rise on the evil and on the good, and sendeth rain on the just and on the unjust.

Van Til writes concerning these verses: "Therefore God's good gifts to men, rain and sunshine in season, are genuinely expressive of God's favor unto them."[3] This is the attitude of most of the Dutch Calvinist writers on the subject, with the exception of the Protestant Reformed Church. It is against this viewpoint that I am arguing.

In a sense, however, Van Til and I are trying to get to the same conclusion: a biblical explanation for God's eternal judgment against specific unregenerate men. We are both trying to deal with history and its eternal consequences for individuals. To put it another way, we are trying to explain the process of historical differentiation and its eternal consequences. This is not some abstract theological question. Some people go to heaven; some people go to

---

3. Cornelius Van Til, *A Letter on Common Grace*, reprinted in *Common Grace and the Gospel* (Nutley, New Jersey: Presbyterian & Reformed, 1974), p. 189.

hell. The question then must be raised: "After death, does God give specific rewards (in heaven) and specific punishments (in hell) to particular people?" If not, why not? If so, then why? A better understanding of the debate over common grace helps us to find correct answers to this down-to-earth (or down even farther) question.

Van Til uses the idea of the common favor of God as the historical background of the specific rebellious lives of individuals. Speaking of Adam, Van Til writes that "man is always reacting ethically to this revelation of God. He first lives under the *general favor* of God and reacts favorably. Then he reacts unfavorably and comes under the curse of God. So far as his ethical attitude is concerned this is in principle entirely hostile to God. Then grace comes on the scene, both saving and non-saving grace."[4] Again, "In particular, man could not be totally depraved if he were not totally enveloped by the revelation of God . . . [A]postasy does not take place in a vacuum."[5] In short, Van Til asks, if the sinner does not have God's *favor* to react against throughout his life, how can he fully develop his own particular historical destiny, and thereby work out his own damnation with or without fear and trembling? This is the question I also ask, but I answer it without making use of the idea of the supposed general favor of God.

---

4. *A Reply to Criticism*, in *ibid.*, p. 207. He says that he is summarizing Calvin here. Van Til's summaries of other Reformed writers' concerns have a tendency to sound as though those writers were somehow working with Van Til's categories.

5. *"Reformed Dogmatics" of Herman Hoeksema*, in *ibid.*, p. 218.

I would argue even more concretely that if there were no *specific gifts* to specific individuals, they could not develop their own historical destinies. We must be careful in our language. We must not call these specific gifts specific or special grace, for special grace is redemptive grace, meaning eternally saving grace. This form of grace is given only to God's elect, "According as he hath chosen us in him before the foundation of the world" (Eph. 1:4a). I argue that we must explain these *specific gifts in history* as manifestations of God's *common grace throughout history*. Common grace is therefore a form of long-term (eternal) curse to the rebellious, and a long-term (eternal) blessing to the righteous.

The sun shines and the rain falls on all men. This is a manifestation of the common grace of God. But Jesus was not simply supplying us with a common-sense theory of the weather. Meteorology was not the central focus of His concern. He was making an *ethical and judicial* point: "But I say unto you, Love your enemies, bless them that curse you, do good to them that hate you, and pray for them which despitefully use you, and persecute you; That ye may be the children of your Father which is in heaven: for he maketh his sun to rise on the evil and on the good, and sendeth rain on the just and on the unjust" (Matthew 5:44-45).

What was His point? *The common blessings of the weather point to the common law of God.* God's blessings must always be seen in terms of God's general covenant with mankind, and this covenant always in-

volves biblical law.[6] What Jesus was saying was that
His people must deal with unbelievers in terms of
biblical law, just as God deals with them. Love means
the fulfilling of the law toward all men (Rom. 13:8).

It is understandable how such verses, in the absence of other verses that more fully explain the
nature and intent of God's gifts, could lead men to
equate God's favor and gifts. Certainly it is true that
God protects, heals, rewards, and cares for the unregenerate. *But none of these verses indicates an attitude of
favor toward the unregenerate beneficiaries of His gifts*. The
attitude of favor is simply *assumed* by Van Til and the
Synod of 1924. Only in the use of the word "favor" in
its English slang form of "do me a favor" can we
argue that a gift from God is the same as His favor.
Favor, in the slang usage, simply means *gift* — an unmerited gift from the donor. But if favor is understood as an attitude favorable to the unregenerate, or
an emotional commitment by God to the unregenerate for their sakes, then it must be said, God shows
no favor to the unrighteous.

Coals of Fire

One verse in the Bible, above all others, informs
us of the underlying attitude of God toward those
who rebel against Him after having received His
gifts. This passage is the concomitant to the oft-
quoted Luke 6:35-36 and Matthew 5:44-45. It is
Proverbs 25:21-22, which Paul cites in Romans 12:20:

---

6. Ray Sutton, *That You May Prosper: Dominion By Covenant* (Ft.
Worth: Dominion Press, 1986). Sutton shows that the third
aspect of the covenant is law, meaning ethics.

If thine enemy be hungry, give him bread
to eat; and if he be thirsty, give him water to
drink: For thou shalt heap coals of fire upon
his head, and the Lord shall reward thee.

Why are we to be kind to our enemies? First, because God instructs us to be kind. He is graciously
kind to them, and we are to imitate Him. Second, by
showing mercy, we thereby heap coals of fire on their
rebellious heads. From him to whom much is given,
much shall be required (Luke 12:47-48). Our enemy
will receive greater punishment through all eternity
because we have been merciful to him. Third, we
are promised a reward from God, which is always a
solid reason for being obedient to His commands.
The language could not be any plainer. Any discussion of common grace which omits Proverbs 25:21-22
(Romans 12:20) from consideration is a misleading
and incomplete discussion of the topic. And I hasten
to point out, Van Til never mentions it.

Love and Hate in Biblical Law

The Bible is very clear. The problem with the
vast majority of interpreters is that they still are influenced by the standards of self-proclaimed autonomous humanism. Biblically, *love is the fulfilling of the
law* (Rom. 13:8). Love thy neighbor, we are instructed. Treat him with respect. Do not oppress or
cheat him. Do not covet his goods or his wife. Do not
steal from him. In treating him lawfully, you have
fulfilled the commandment to love him. In so doing,
you have rendered him without excuse on the day of

judgment. God's people are to become conduits of God's gifts to the unregenerate. We must be gracious, for God is gracious.

But never forget: we must hate God's enemies as He hates them. This hatred must always take place within the confines of biblical law. We must love, and we must hate. The two are equally ultimate.

Let me raise a key question, which the reader may already have thought of. "How can holy hate operate within the framework of biblical law, if love is the fulfilling of the law?" At this point, we come to the hidden genius of biblical law. It is an instrument of grace and also an instrument of condemnation. This is Paul's message in Romans 6-8. It kills, but it can lead to life if God regenerates the law-cursed sinner. At the cross, the law became the basis of Christ's condemnation as well as our deliverance. We are to obey biblical law, for it is simultaneously an instrument of destruction against God's enemies and an instrument of reconstruction for God's kingdom.

We act lawfully toward our enemies, always bearing in mind this two-fold aspect of law. Like the covenant, biblical law has two sides: blessing and cursing. We are not to imagine that every good gift that we give to the lost must be given in an attempt to heap coals of fire on their heads. We do not know God's plan for the ages, except in its broad outlines. We do not know who God intends to redeem. So we give freely, hoping that some might be redeemed and the others damned. We play our part in the salvation of some and the damnation of others. For example, regenerate marriage partners are explicitly instructed to treat their unregenerate partners lawfully and faithfully. "For what knowest thou, O wife, whether thou shalt save thy husband? or how knowest thou, O man, whether thou shalt save thy wife?" (I Cor. 7:16).

God says that we must treat our friends and enemies lawfully, for they are made in the image of God. But we are to understand that our honest treatment makes it *far worse* on the day of judgment for those unrepentant sinners with whom we have dealt righteously than if we had disobeyed God and been poor testimonies to them, treating them unlawfully. They have rebelled against a greater specific manifestation of God's grace to them. From him to whom more is given, more is expected. Since this extra gratefulness is not forthcoming from them, their punishment is greater, for all eternity. Some sinners will be brought to eternal salvation as a result of God's earthly grace to them by means of our gift of lawful dealing, while others will be brought to a more severe eternal condemnation as a result of God's earthly grace to them by means of our gift.

God gives ethical rebels enough rope to hang themselves for all eternity. This is a fundamental implication of the doctrine of common grace. The law of God condemns some men, yet it simultaneously serves as a means of repentance and salvation for others (Rom. 5:19-20). The same law produces different results in different people. What separates men ethically and eternally is the saving grace of God in election. The law of God serves as a tool of final *destruction* against the lost, yet it also serves as a tool of active *reconstruc-*

tion for the Christian. The law rips up the kingdom of Satan, just as it serves as the foundation for the kingdom of God on earth.

Equal Ultimacy, Unequal Effects

Just as the idea of eternal punishment is equally ultimate in the covenant as the idea of eternal blessing, so is the idea of temporal destruction equally ultimate with temporal reconstruction. But there is this difference: reconstruction is a positive process, and expands its influence over time. Destruction is negative. In hell, it may or may not be that men increase in their rebellion throughout eternity, learning new ways to resent God and curse him. I do not know. But in the perfect consummation of the New Heaven and New Earth after resurrection day, men will learn ever more about God and His creation, as finite creatures working to understand the infinite. Redeemed men will heap new praises to God throughout eternity as they learn more of His glory. He is infinitely good; there will always be more to praise. In short, when it comes to the glory of God, "there's plenty more where that came from."

Thus, while election and reprobation, blessing and cursing, resurrection unto eternal life and resurrection unto the second death (Rev. 20:14) are *equally ultimate in principle* in the covenant, *they are not equally ultimate in their respective effects in eternity.* The manifestation of God's glory is positive in the post-resurrection New Heavens and New Earth, and negative in the eternal lake of fire. The manifestation of God's glory is progressive (developing) in a positive feedback sense in the consummated New Heavens and New Earth. (Notice that I keep saying the *consummated* New Heavens and New Earth. We are now living in the pre-consummation New Heavens and New Earth: Isa. 65:17-20. This, too, is marked by positive feedback.)

The manifestation of God's eternal glory in wrathfulness may or may not develop in the lake of fire, in response to some sort of developing negative rebellion in the lake of fire; we are not told. But it is certain that the lake of fire does not drift toward "non-being." It is eternal. Its impotence perhaps will be locked in place at the day of judgment — no "negative dominion," no post-resurrection development of skills in rebelliousness. (I rather suspect that this is the case.) But clearly, the residents of the lake of fire will go nowhere and accomplish nothing by means of power. Satan rules in hell today; he will only fry in the lake of fire. His single mark of final distinction will be the temperature at which he is fried: "first among equals." This, however, points to God's common grace to Satan throughout history. He has received great power in history; he will receive great judgment in eternity. From him to whom much has been given, much is expected. He who rebels against greater gifts from God is going to suffer greater punishment than he who has revolted against fewer gifts (Luke 12:47-48).

We see in Satan and his followers the working out of the dual principle: equal ultimacy (total depravity of all rebels), but with unequal effects (appropriate judgment in terms of the individual's works in relation to the grace that God has shown to him in history). We also see in Christ and his followers the working out of this same dual principle: equal ultimacy (the perfect humanity of Christ imputed to all redeemed men), but with unequal effects (appropriate judgment in terms of the individual's works in relation to the grace that God has shown to him in history).

What I am arguing in this book is that the two aspects of the covenant — blessing and cursing — are not equally ultimate in their respective *effects* in history, just as they are not equal in their eternal effects. Different individuals experience different histories, depending on the extent to which they affirm or deny the covenant by their actions. Similarly, different societies experience different histories, depending on the extent to which they affirm or deny the covenant by their actions.

The working out of the principle of covenantal blessing can lead to the positive feedback operation: historical blessing to covenantal reaffirmation to greater historical blessing . . . (Deut. 8:18). (A theonomic postmillennialist should argue that it *does* eventually operate in history in this fashion, leading to millennial blessings.) The working out of covenantal cursing leads to temporal scattering and destruction (Deut. 8:19-20). Every Christian theologian admits that the working out of covenantal cursing in history eventually leads to final destruction for God's enemies. Theologians debate only about the historical path of this development to final judgment: premillennial, amillennial, or postmillennial.

Consistent Living

As I argue throughout this book, it is only be-cause ethical rebels are *not* fully self-consistent his-torically in their ethical rebellion that they can main-tain power (an external gift from God). If they were fully self-consistent, they would without exception all commit suicide, for all those who hate God love death (Prov. 8:36b). A fully self-consistent ethical rebel could be no threat to God or God's people if they were also fully self-consistent, as we will see throughout eternity.

Christians are supposed to become more consist-ent with the religion they profess. They are to imi-tate the perfect humanity (but not the divinity) of Jesus Christ. It is only because God's people are not yet fully self-consistent ethically that they need the services of sinners (the division of labor) in history — sinners who are themselves not fully self-consistent ethically. After the resurrection, both groups are allowed by God to become fully consistent ethically, and therefore they must be separated from each other eternally. God wins, Satan loses. We win, they lose. End of argument. End of ethical inconsistency.

When God at last is ready to judge mankind, and make ethically perfect all His saints, then He perma-nently separates the saved from the lost. Perfect saints will no longer need to rely on the productivity of the rebels. The ethical rebels will no longer need to be restrained by God in the working out of their anti-God presuppositions. God's restraint and His gifts to the rebels then cease. He sends fire upon them (Rev. 20:9). History will end because the

Christians will have come so close to self-consistent
living that rebels cannot stand to live close to them.
So God will at last separate the wheat from the tares.
This is the central theme of this book.

Favor to Satan?

The idea that God shows favor to ethical rebels
eventually comes into conflict with the idea of God's
gifts to Satan, which are said by the defenders of the
1924 Synod not to involve God's favor. They have to
admit that God gives Satan gifts. There is no question that the grace of God in extending temporal life
to mankind after the rebellion of Adam also involved
extending time to Satan and his angels. There is no
question that the grace of God in extending all other
temporal blessings to mankind after the rebellion of
Adam—knowledge, law, power, peace, etc.—also
involved extending these same blessings to Satan
and his angels. If nothing else, Satan is empowered
by God to establish satanic covenants with his followers, covenants that bear four of the five marks of
God's covenant.[7]

All of life is covenantal. The battles of life are
therefore covenantal. Anything that happens to
those who are under God's covenant affects the

---

7. The five aspects of God's covenant, as Sutton shows in *That
You May Prosper*, are these: (1) transcendence/immanence (the
presence of God), (2) hierarchy/authority (organization), (3)
law/ethics (dominion), (4) judicial (evaluational), and (5) inheritance (continuity). Satan's covenants lack only the first, for he is
not divine and omnipresent. He compensates for this lack by
creating a centralized top-down hierarchy in place of God's
bottom-up appeals court covenantal structure.

working out in history of God's covenantal church. Anything that happens to those who are under Satan's covenant also affects the working out of Satan's covenantal anti-church. When God extends gifts to all men, he thereby extends gifts to Satan's covenantal anti-church. If Satan's earthly troops fare well, then to that extent, Satan also fares well — of course, leading always to Satan's eternal farewell.

There can be no discussion of God's gifts to men in general without a discussion of God's grace to Satan. To the extent that human language can express reality, the same kinds of gifts that God extends to mankind in general are also extended to Satan and his demonic host: time, law, power, knowledge, etc.

This raises a very real problem for Van Til. How can he assert that God's common grace demonstrates God's *favor* to all men in some sense, without it leading him to the obvious conclusion, namely, that God's common grace also demonstrates God's favor in some sense to Satan?

Van Til never deals with this problem in a straightforward manner. This is understandable, since his Christian Reformed interpretation of common grace is threatened by this fundamental question. He does assert that Satan is not an object of God's favor. He says this in relation to his rejection of Dutch theologian Klaas Schilder's view of common grace.

Van Til vs. Schilder

Schilder, a brilliant Dutch theologian, was asked by a Christian Reformed writer in 1939, fifteen years after the 1924 Synod, to offer his opinions concerning the 1924 formulation of common grace. Schilder rejected point one, as I do, and as the Protestant Reformed Church did and still does. Schilder recognized that if God's common grace is defined as God's favor to unregenerate men, then there is no way to distinguish God's favor to mankind from favor to the creation in general. He therefore rejected the wording of the Synod's first point. He rejected the notion that God shows favor to "creatures in general," including the non-elect. "Creatures in general," Schilder said, includes fallen angels. Van Til summarizes: "And God certainly is not favorable to devils."[8] This is the crux of the matter.

But Van Til, not wanting to break with the 1924 Synod, avoids the crux. Instead, he launches into one of his rambling philosophical digressions for several pages on why we must reinterpret what Schilder is saying, why we must reject what Schilder is saying, and what the Synod "meant to say." It includes the familiar references to Plato, Arminianism, the "full-bucket difficulty," brute facts, rationalism vs. irrationalism, analogical reasoning, neutrality, and so forth. The following sample is representative:

> For better or worse Synod meant to teach that God has a certain attitude of favor to all men as men. The use of the broad popular phrase "creatures in general" gives no justification for drawing such consequences as Schilder has drawn. Besides, the broad phrase itself ex-

---

8. Van Til, *Common Grace*, in *Common Grace and the Gospel*, p. 26

presses the fact that God loves all His creatures. And as for the idea that God loves all
creatureliness as such, including the creatureliness of the devil, this is, we believe, intelligible
only if we use it as a limiting concept.[9]

A *limiting concept*? Shades of Immanuel Kant. If
this is what the Synod "meant to teach," then it
should have waited to say what it meant in clear language that normal God-fearing people can understand, rather than rushing a poorly worded statement through the bureaucracy, and driving out a
man of the stature of Herman Hoeksema and thousands of his followers.

When you face both Herman Hoeksema and
Klaas Schilder in theological debate, you had better
have your arguments ready. In this instance, Van
Til didn't have them ready. Van Til is quibbling—
quibbling desperately. The fact is, the Synod was
wrong, and all the "limiting concepts" in the world
will not make what it said correct. God gives gifts to
Satan. God shows no favor to Satan. It does not take
a Ph.D. in philosophy or a Th.D. in theology to
make the obvious conclusion. God also gives gifts to
the non-elect, covenanted disciples of Satan. God
also shows no favor to the non-elect, covenanted followers of Satan.

I do not want to bury myself or the reader in the
subtleties and qualifications of Schilder's argument,

9. *Idem.*

as summarized by Van Til. Perhaps Schilder made
some technical philosophical errors. He is dead, and
the 1924 Synod is not much healthier. So let us deal
with Van Til, whose arguments are still alive.

He has two ways to escape this conclusion that
the 1924 Synod's statement leads to the conclusion
that God shows favor to Satan. First, he could abandon the Christian Reformed Church's first point,
and stop speaking of the common grace of God as
God's favor. This he refuses to do. Second, he could
assert that there is a fundamental difference between
God's common grace to mankind in general, and His
extension of time, knowledge, law, power, etc. to
Satan. In principle, he takes this second approach,
but never clearly and never with a detailed explanation, for *the exegetical and logical means of making this distinction between gifts to mankind and the same gifts to Satan
do not exist.*

Making Indistinct Distinctions

Van Til cannot make the distinction by an appeal
to the image of God in man, which Satan does not
possess. Van Til quite correctly argues that the image of God in man is essential to the very being of
man, and it never departs, even in eternity: ". . . as
a creature made in God's image, man's constitution
as a rational and moral being has *not* been destroyed.
The separation from God on the part of the sinner is
ethical. . . . Even the lost in the hereafter have not
lost the power of rational and moral determination.
They must have this image in order to be aware of

their lost condition."[10] Men are men eternally.

Common grace, and therefore God's supposed common favor toward mankind in general, is exclusively an aspect of history. "When history is finished God no longer has any kind of favor toward the reprobate. They still exist and God has pleasure in their existence, but not in the fact of their bare existence. God has pleasure in their historically *defeated* existence."[11]

So it cannot be the fact that Satan is not made in God's image that disqualifies him from the favor of God. Reprobate men in eternity are disqualified, too. The issue is historical, not the image of God in man. So what is it in Satan that disqualifies him from God's supposed favor in general? Why is the creation in general, including Satan, not the recipient of God's favor?

Van Til must distinguish favor to *mankind in general* in history from favor to *creatures in general* in history, if he is to preserve his distinction between favor to mankind and no favor to Satan. Could it be that Satan is totally evil now, and that his evil does not develop in history? Is his evil in principle identical to his evil at every point in time? Is he in this sense non-historical, and therefore not the object of God's favor?

Satan and History

Van Til writes little about Satan, but in the few pages of his *Introduction to Systematic Theology* in which

---

10. *A Reply to Criticism*, in *ibid.*, p. 198.
11. *Common Grace*, in *ibid.*, p. 30.

he discusses Satan, he closes this possible escape
hatch. Satan is a historical creature, he says. "It is
true, of course, that when Cain left the face of the
Lord, he in a sense knew God just as well as he knew
him just before. It is true also that there is a sense in
which Satan knows God now as well as he knew God
before the fall. In a sense, Satan knows God better
now than before. Did not God prove the truth of his
statements to Satan thousands of times? But herein
exactly lies the contradiction of Satan's personality
that though he knows God yet he does not really
know God. His very intellect is constantly devising
schemes by which he thinks he may overthrow God,
while he knows all too well that God cannot be overthrown. What else can this be but a manifestation of
the wrath of God? Yes, it was the natural consequence of sin, but this is itself the wrath of God, that
sin should be allowed to run its course. In like manner, too, man's thought since the entrance of sin has
been characterized by *self-frustration*."[12]

Satan rebels again and again in history. He is a
creature of history just as surely as his covenanted
human followers are creatures of history. Cain, like
Satan, learned more about God in his escalating rebellion. Yet Cain was the beneficiary of God's favor,
Van Til must argue, during the time he operated in
history. Satan is still operating in history, too. So
why deny God's common favor to Satan?

Does Satan learn from history? Yes, he learns that
opposition to God is fruitless. Van Til insists that

12. *Introduction to Systematic Theology*, Vol. V of *In Defense of the
Faith* (Phillipsburg, New Jersey: Presbyterian and Reformed,
1974), p. 92.

Satan learns more about God in history: ". . . Satan himself must have become increasingly convinced that God is God in the sense that he is absolute. . . ."[13] Rebellious man's knowledge of God is not different in principle from Satan's: "In spite of all this, man has not accepted for himself what he himself must admit to be the true interpretation of the origin of the world. In this respect man's knowledge is characterized by the same folly that marks Satan's knowledge of God."[14] Fallen man's knowledge is like Satan's. Then why deny God's favor to Satan in history?

Van Til has closed off most of his available loopholes. He relies on one final possibility. Satan's knowledge of God, he writes, is less clouded than man's. This passage in *Introduction to Systematic Theology* he also cites in *A Letter on Common Grace*, so he must regard it as the key. (It appears on page 94 of the *Introduction*, not on page 98, as he mistakenly says.)

> Here we should again bring in the fact of the non-saving grace of God. In the case of Satan, the folly of his interpretation [of God and history—G.N.] appears very clear. In the case of the sinner, however, we have a mixed situation. Through God's non-saving grace, the wrath of God on the sinner has been mitigated in this life. . . . He is not a finished product.[15]

---

13. *Idem.*
14. *Ibid.*, p. 94.
15. *A Letter on Common Grace*, in *Common Grace and the Gospel*, p. 165.

Here is Van Til's distinction between Satan and man. Satan has a clear revelation of the folly of his interpretation; man does not. Man is not a finished product, Van Til writes; the obvious (but unstated) conclusion must be that Satan is a finished product. The reader is led to ask: "In what way is Satan a finished product and man isn't?" Here is where Van Til needs to clarify what he means. He never does.

Satan grows in the knowledge of God. So does man. Satan rebels against ever-greater quantities of revelation as history progresses. So does man. Satan is judged at the final judgment. So is man. Satan has been given time, knowledge, power, and all the other gifts given to man. So wherein lies the fundamental difference? Why aren't unmerited gifts from God to Satan proof of God's favor to Satan, if God's gifts of unmerited gifts to unregenerate men *are* proof of His common favor?

Van Til never says. I think it is because he cannot say, and still maintain the Christian Reformed Church's equating of common grace and common favor.

Pounding the Podium

There is an old debater's trick that says: "When your argument is weak, pound the podium and shout."

Van Til never ceases asserting (without exegetical evidence) that the common favor of God is the biblical position.

How can God have an attitude of favor unto those who are according to His own ultimate will to be separated from him forever? The first and basic answer is that Scripture teaches it.[16]

There are those who have denied common grace. They have argued that God *cannot* have any attitude of favor at *any stage* in history to such as are the "vessels of wrath." But to reason this way is to make logic rule over Scripture.[17]

Scholasticism appears when, on the ground of the idea of election, we deduce that God cannot in any sense whatever have any favor to mankind as a group.[18]

These are assertions, not arguments. Van Til never offers systematically exegetical arguments defending common grace as common favor. He simply repeats over and over that the Christian Reformed Church's view is the biblical view.

Common Grace Without Favor

The proper view is something very different. God's common grace implies no favor to the lost in history. Therefore, God's common grace can be said to extend to Satan. Satan's forces, both demonic and human, receive unmerited gifts from God. Christ died for the whole created world (John 3:16), including Satan. He did not die in order that the offer of salvation be made to Satan. No such offer is ever made. The offer of eternal life goes only to men.

---

16. *Common Grace and Witness-Bearing*, in *ibid.*, p. 140.
17. *A Letter on Common Grace*, in *ibid.*, p. 165.
18. *A Reply to Criticism*, in *ibid.*, p. 200.

It is possible to argue that in this sense, the death of Christ for Satan differs from the death of Christ for unregenerate people. But however the theologians want to debate this difference, it clearly has to do with some aspect of special (soul-saving) grace, not common grace. The distinction applies to the free offer of the gospel to men and not to Satan; it does not apply to the common gifts of life, knowledge, law, power, etc.

The unmerited gifts from God serve to condemn both the unregenerate and Satan and his angels. These gifts do not imply favor. They simply are means of heaping coals of fire on rebellious heads, human and demonic.

Conclusion

Christ is indeed the savior of all people prior to the day of judgment (I Tim. 4:10). Christ sustains the whole universe (Col. 1:17). Without Him, no living thing could survive. He grants to His creatures such gifts as *time, law, order, power,* and *knowledge.* He grants all of these gifts to Satan and his rebellious host. The answer to the question, "Does God show His grace and mercy to all creation, including Satan?" is emphatically *yes*. Satan is given time and power to do his evil work. To the next question, "Does this mean that God in some way demonstrates an attitude of favor toward Satan?" the answer is emphatically *no*. God is no more favorable toward Satan and his demons than he is to Satan's human followers. But this does not mean that He does not bestow gifts upon them — gifts that they in no way deserve.

Thus, the doctrine of common grace must apply not only to men but also to Satan and the fallen angels. This is what Van Til denies, because he defines common grace as *favor in general* rather than *gifts in general*. The second concept does not imply the first.

God does not favor "mankind" as such. He showers favors on all men, but this does not mean that He favors men in general. Men in general rebelled against Him in the garden. Adam and Eve, mankind's representatives, brought the entire human race under God's wrath. God in His grace gave them time and covenant promises, for He looked forward to the death of His Son on the cross. On this basis, and only on this basis, men have been given life in history. Some have been given life in order to extend God's kingdom, while others have been given life (like Pharaoh) to demonstrate God's power, and to heap coals of fire eternally on their heads.

In summary:

1. God hated Esau before he was born: no favor.
2. God gives gifts to the unregenerate.
3. God heals them as a savior (I Tim. 4:10).
4. We are required to love our enemies.
5. This means we must deal with them lawfully.
6. God tells us to deal lawfully with evil men in order to heap coals of fire on their heads.
7. Lawful dealing by us will lead some men to Christ.

8. God gives evil people enough rope to hang themselves eternally.

9. Biblical law is a tool: of destruction against Satan's kingdom and reconstruction by Christians.

10. God is not favorable to Satan and demons.

11. God nevertheless gives them time and power.

12. He does the same with Satan's human followers.

13. Blessing and cursing are equally ultimate in the covenant.

14. The manifestations of blessing and cursing are not equally ultimate in impact.

15. Satan's knowledge and evil increase over time.

2

GOD'S RESTRAINING HAND VS. TOTAL DEPRAVITY

To deliver such an one unto Satan for the destruction of the flesh, that the spirit may be saved in the day of the Lord Jesus (I Cor. 5:5).

Why did Paul require the Corinthian church to cast the incestuous person out of the church? To deliver him into the power of Satan. Later, the man did return to the church; the church's discipline of excommunication worked to restore a lost sinner to His God (II Cor. 2:6-11).

God did the same thing with Israel time after time, and for the same reason. When they worshipped foreign gods, He delivered them into the hands of cruel foreign nations that worshipped those gods. As James Jordan writes of the periods of bondage described in the Book of Judges: "Israel had become enslaved to the Canaanite Gods; it was therefore logical and necessary that they also become enslaved to the Canaanite culture. In effect God said, 'So you like the gods of Ammon? Well then, you're going to just love being under Ammonite culture!' "[1] He did this in order to break their rebellion and get them to return to Him. "Oh, you don't like being in bondage to Ammon? You'd like to have Me as your God once again? Wonderful, I'll send a Judge, who will have My Son as his Captain, and set you free from Ammon."[2]

God in His grace refuses to allow men in history to walk fully consistently with their own evil hearts. But in His wrath, He may give them more "slack" on His chain of restraint, allowing them to impose a wider circle of destruction. He does this as a prelude to judgment, either judgment unto restoration (e.g., Israel in Babylon) or judgment unto oblivion (e.g., Sodom). When He lets them go, allowing them in history to approach (though never fully reach) the total, comprehensive depravity in their hearts, He thereby brings them into judgment in history.

Let me say it again: when God releases a person to his own devices, as He did with that sinner in the Corinthian church, He thereby begins to bring him under judgment. He ceases to restrain a person from committing evil. When God ceases to restrain the evil that men want to commit, they will eventually fall under some form of earthly judgment. Perhaps the best example of this is venereal disease. Strict monogamy is the only successful long-term prophylactic against venereal disease. God sometimes re-

---

1. James B. Jordan, *Judges: God's War Against Humanism* (Tyler, Texas: Geneva Ministries, 1985), p. 41.
2. *Idem.*

moves people from the protection of His law, which is designed to restrain evil (Rom. 13:1-7).

Biblical Law Is a Means of Grace

Biblical law is a means of grace: common grace to those who are perishing, special grace to those who are regenerate. We all benefit from God's extension of blessings to us when we are externally faithful to the external terms of the covenant. To use the example of venereal disease again, when most people are monogamous, they are protected from the spread of these killer diseases. Ethical rebels who in other areas of their lives disobey biblical law at least remain free from this particular scourge. Or to use the example in Matthew 5, when God sends good weather, sinners enjoy it too.

Biblical law is also a form of curse: special curse to those who are perishing, common curse to those who are regenerate. We are all under the legal requirements of God's covenant as men, and because of the curse on the creation, we suffer the *temporal* burdens of Adam's transgression. The whole world labors under this curse (Rom. 8:18-23). Nevertheless, "all things work together for good to them that love God, to them who are the called according to his purpose" (Rom. 8:28). The common curse on nature is not a special curse on God's people.

As men, we are all under the law of the covenant and the restraint of its law, both physical and personal law, and we can use this knowledge of law either to bring us external blessings through obedience or to rebel and bring destruction. But we

know also that all things work together for evil for
them that hate God, to them who are the rejected according to His purpose (Rom. 9:17-22). Common
grace — common curse, special grace — special curse:
we must affirm all four.

The Transgression of Biblical Law

The transgression of biblical law brings a *special
curse* to the unregenerate. It is a curse of eternal duration. But this same transgression brings only a *common curse* to God's people. A Christian gets sick, he
suffers losses, he is blown about by the storm, he
suffers sorrow, but he does not suffer the second
death (Rev. 2:11; 20:6, 14). Perhaps his nation suffers
a plague or a military defeat because of the sinfulness of most of his neighbors and his nation's rulers.
For the believer, the common curses of life are God's
chastening, signs of God's favor (Heb. 12:6).

The difference between common curse and special curse is not found in the intensity of human pain
or the extent of any loss; the difference lies in *God's
attitude* toward those who are laboring under the external and psychological burdens. There is an attitude of favor toward God's people, but none toward
the unregenerate. The *common curse of the unregenerate
person* is, in fact, a part of the special curse under
which he will labor forever. The *common curse of the regenerate person* is a part of the special grace in terms of
which he finally prospers.

The common curse is nonetheless common,
despite its differing effects on the eternal state of
men. The law of God is sure. God does not respect
persons (Rom. 2:11), with one exception: the Person

of Jesus Christ. Christ was perfect, yet He was punished. For the sake of all creation, Christ was singled out by God to be mistreated. God "respected" Christ's Person in a unique way by showing *public disrespect* to Christ on the day of the crucifixion and the following day in the grave. He deserted His own righteous Son in public, so Jesus called out, "My God, my God, why hast thou forsaken me?" (Matt. 27:46b). Then came the resurrection.

Restraining Man's Self-Hatred

If the *effects* of biblical law are *common in cursing*, then the effects of biblical law are also *common in grace*. This is why we need a doctrine of common grace. This doctrine gives meaning to the doctrine of common curse, and vice versa. The law of God restrains men in their evil ways, whether regenerate or unregenerate. The law of God restrains "the old man" (Col. 3:8) or old sin nature in Christians. The law's restraint of evil is therefore a true blessing for all men. In fact, it is even a temporary blessing for Satan and his demons. All those who hate God love death (Prov. 8:36b). *This hatred of God and self is restrained during history.* Evil men are given knowledge, law, power, life, and time that they do not deserve. Satan receives these same gifts. But evil creatures cannot fully work out the implications of their rebellious, suicidal faith, for God's lawful restraint will not permit it.

The common grace which restrains the totally depraved character of Satan and all his followers is, in fact, part of God's *special curse* on them. Every gift returns to condemn them on the day of judgment, heaping coals of fire on their heads. On the other hand, the common grace of God in law also must be seen as a part of the program of special grace to His people. God's special gifts to His people, person by person, are the source of varying rewards on the day of judgment (I Cor. 3:11-15). Similarly, common grace serves to condemn the rebels proportionately to the benefits they have received on earth, and it serves as the operating backdrop for the special grace given to God's people.

The laws of God offer a source of order, power, and dominion. Some men use this common grace to their ultimate destruction, while others use it to their eternal benefit. It is nonetheless common, despite its differing effects on the eternal state of men.

The Good That Men Do

The Bible teaches that there is no good thing inherent in fallen man; his heart is wicked and deceitful (Jer. 17:9). All our self-proclaimed righteousness is as filthy rags in the sight of God (Isa. 64:6). Nevertheless, we also know that history has meaning, that there are permanent standards that enable us to distinguish the life of God-hating Communist Joseph Stalin from the life of God-hating pantheist Albert Schweitzer. There are different punishments for different unregenerate men (Luke 12:45-48). This does not mean that God in some way favors one lost soul more than another. It only means that in the eternal plan of God there must be *an eternal affirmation of the validity and permanence of His law*. It is worse to be a murderer than a liar or a thief. Not every sin is a sin unto death, but some are (I John 5:16-17). History is not some amorphous, undifferentiated mass. It is not an illusion. It has implications for eternity. Therefore, the law of God stands as a reminder to unregenerate men that it is better to conform in part than not to conform at all, even though the end result of rebellion is destruction. There are degrees of punishment according to men's knowledge (Luke 12:47-48).

God restrains the *innate and total depravity* of man in history. Van Til writes: "However, God not only gives good gifts to men in general, He not only calls men with the good news of the gospel to a renewed acceptance of their original task, He also restrains the wrath of man. He keeps the negative, and therefore destructive, force of sin from breaking out in the fulness of its powers. All men everywhere are kept from working out self-consciously their own adopted principle as covenant-breakers and as children of wrath. But none of them have reached maturity in sinning."[3] Because of this restraint, evil men can do good things: "And in restraining him in his ethical hostility to God, God releases his creaturely powers so that he can make positive contributions to the field of knowledge and art." This benefits redeemed men through the division of labor. People who are spiritually evil can nevertheless perform morally good acts: "Similarly, in restraining him from expressing his ethical hostility to God there is a release

---

3. Van Til, *Particularism and Common Grace*, in *Common Grace and the Gospel*, p. 117.

within him of his moral powers so that they can perform that which is 'morally' though not spiritually good."[4]

But what is the source of the good that evil men do? It can be no other than God (James 1:17). He is the source of all good. He restrains men in different ways, and the effects of this restraint, person to person, demon to demon, can be seen throughout all eternity. Not favor toward the unregenerate, but rather perfect justice of law and total respect toward the law of God on the part of God Himself are the sources of the good deeds that men who are lost may accomplish in time and on earth.

The Knowledge of the Law

The work of the law is written on every man's heart. There is no escape. No man can plead ignorance (Rom. 2:11-14). But each man's history does have meaning, and some men have been given clearer knowledge than others (Luke 12:47-48). There is a *common knowledge* of the law, yet there is also *special knowledge* of the law—historically unique in the life of each man. Each man will be judged by the deeds that he has done, by every word that he has uttered (Rom. 2:6; Matt. 12:36). God testifies to His faithfulness to His word by distinguishing every shade of evil and good in every man's life, saved or lost.

Time for the Canaanites

Perhaps a biblical example can clarify these issues. God gave the people who dwelt in the land of

---

4. *A Letter on Common Grace, ibid.*, p. 174.

Canaan an extra generation of sovereignty over their land. The slave mentality of the Hebrews, with the exceptions of Joshua and Caleb, did not permit them to go in and conquer the land. Israel's sinfulness became a factor in Canaan's history: the basis of a stay of execution. Furthermore, God specifically revealed to Israel that He would drive the Canaanites out, city by city, year by year, so that the wild animals could not take over the land, leaving it desolate (Ex. 23:27-30).

Did this reveal God's favor toward the Canaanites? Hardly. He instructed the Hebrews to destroy them, root and branch. They were to be driven out of their land forever (Ex. 23:32-33). Nevertheless, they did receive a temporal blessing: an extra generation or more of peace. This kept the beasts in their place. It allowed the Hebrews to mature under the law of God. It also allowed the Hebrews to heap coals of fire on the heads of their enemies, for as God told Abraham, the Hebrews would not take control of the promised land in his day, "for the iniquity of the Amorites is not yet full" (Gen. 15:16). During that final generation, the iniquity of the Amorites was filled to the brim. Then came destruction.

The Canaanites did receive more than they deserved. They stayed in the land of their fathers for an extra generation. Were they beneficiaries? Yes. During the days of wandering for the Hebrews, the Canaanites were beneficiaries. Then the final payment, culturally speaking, came due, and it was exacted by God through His people, just as the Egyptians had learned to their woe. They cared for the land until the Hebrews were fit to take possession of it. As the Bible affirms, "the wealth of the sinner is laid up for the just" (Prov. 13:22b). But this in no way denies the value of the sinner's wealth during the period in which he controls it. It is a gift from God that he has anything at all. God has restrained sinners from dispersing their wealth in a flurry of suicidal destruction. He lets them serve as caretakers until the day that it is transferred to the regenerate.

The Gibeonites did escape destruction. They were wise enough to see that God's people could not be beaten. They tricked Joshua into making a treaty with them. The result was their perpetual bondage as menial laborers, but they received life, and the right to pursue happiness, although they forfeited liberty. They were allowed to live under the restraints of God's law, a far better arrangement culturally than they had lived under before the arrival of the Hebrews. They became the recipients of the cultural blessings given to the Hebrews, and perhaps some of them became faithful to God. In that case, what had been a curse on all of them — servitude — became a means of special grace. Their deception paid off (Josh. 9). Only these Hivites of Gibeon escaped destruction (Josh. 11:20).

Time for Adam and Eve

In the day that Adam and Eve ate of the tree of knowledge, they died spiritually. God had told them they would die on that very day. But they did not die physically. They may or may not have been individually regenerated by God's Spirit, but they were unquestionably the beneficiaries of a promise (Gen. 3:15). They were to be allowed to have children. Before time began, God had ordained the crucifixion. Christ was in this sense slain from the very beginning (Rev. 13:8). God therefore granted Adam and Eve time on earth. He extended their lease on life; had they not sinned, they would have been able to own eternal life. God greatly blessed them and their murderous son Cain with a stay of execution. God respected Christ's work on the cross. Christ became a savior to Cain — not a personal savior or regenerating savior, but a savior of his life. God granted Cain protection (Gen. 4:15), one of the tasks of a savior.

Meaning in History

Once again, we see that history has meaning. History has meaning and purpose because God has a plan for history. God has a decree. He grants favors to rebels, but not because He is favorable to them. He respects His Son, and His Son died for the whole world (John 3:16). He died to save the world, meaning to give it additional time, life, and external blessings — more than it deserved. He died to become a savior in the same sense as that described in the first part of I Timothy 4:10 — not a special savior, but a sustaining, restraining savior. God dealt mercifully with Adam and Adam's family because He had favor for His chosen people, those who receive the blessings of salvation. But that salvation is expressly *historical* in nature. Christ died in history for His people. They are regenerated in history. For their sake, He therefore preserves the earth and gives all men, including ethical rebels, additional time.

With respect to God's restraint of the total depravity of men, consider His curse of the ground (Gen. 3:17-19). Man must labor in the sweat of his brow in order to eat. The earth gives up her fruits, but only through labor. Still, this common curse also involves common grace. Men are compelled to cooperate with each other in a world of scarcity if they wish to increase their income. They may be murderers in their hearts, but they must restrain their emotions and cooperate. The division of labor makes possible the specialization of production. This, in turn, promotes increased wealth for all those who labor. Men are restrained by scarcity, which appears to be a one-sided curse. Not so; it is equally a blessing.[5] This is the meaning of common grace: common curse and common grace go together until the final judgment. After that, there is no more common grace or common curse. There is eternal separation.

The cross is the best example of the fusion of grace and curse. Christ was totally cursed on the cross. At the same time, this was God's act of incomparable grace. Justice and mercy are linked at the cross. Christ died, thereby experiencing the curse common to all men. Yet through that death, Christ propitiated God's wrath. The cross is the source of common grace on earth—life, law, order, power—as well as the source of special grace.

---

5. Gary North, *The Dominion Covenant: Genesis* (Tyler, Texas: Institute for Christian Economics, 1982), ch. 10: "Scarcity: Curse and Blessing."

The *common curse* of the cross — death that is common to all mankind — led to *special grace* for God's people, yet it also is the source of additional time: *common grace* which makes history possible. Christ's common curse on the cross (physical death) and His special curse (separation from God)[6] led to the special grace of salvation to God's people, and the common grace of life. The cross is therefore the source of life — common grace. Christ suffered the "first death" and the "second death" (separation), not to save His people from the first death (for every person dies), and not to save the unregenerate from the second death of the lake of fire (Rev. 20:14). He suffered the first death and the second death to satisfy the penalty of sin — the first death (which Adam did not immediately pay, since he did not die physically on the day that he sinned) and also the second death (God's people will never perish).

"Let Go, and Let Satan"

At some time in the future, God will cease to restrain men's evil (II Thess. 2:6-12). Just as He gave up Israel to their lusts (Ps. 81:12; 106:15), so shall He give up the unregenerate who are presently held back from part of the evil that they would do. This does not necessarily mean that the unregener-

---

6. This separation took place before His physical death, when He cried out, "My God, my God, why hast thou forsaken me?" At His death, He did not go to hell, or at least not for very long (assuming the Apostles' creed is correct: "He descended into hell," meaning literal hell rather than merely the grave). He told the thief on the other cross, "To day shalt thou be with me in paradise" (Luke 23:43).

ate will then crush the people of God. In fact, it means precisely the opposite.

When God ceased to restrain the sins of Israel, Israel grew very evil, and then was invaded, defeated, and scattered. The very act of releasing them from His restraint allowed God to let them fill up their own cup of iniquity. The end result of God's releasing Israel was their fall into iniquity, rebellion, and impotence (Acts 7:42-43). They were scattered by the Assyrians, the Babylonians, and finally the Romans. The Christian church thereby became the heir to God's kingdom (Matt. 21:43). The Romans, too, were given up to their own lusts (Rom. 1:24, 26, 28). Though it took three centuries, they were finally replaced by the Christians. The pagan Roman empire collapsed. The Christians picked up the pieces.[7]

When God ceases to restrain men from the evil that they are capable of committing, this seals their doom. Separated from restraint, they violate *the work of the law* that is written in their hearts (Rom. 2:14-15). Rebelling against God's law, men lose God's tool of cultural dominion. Men who see themselves as being under law can then use the law to achieve their ends. Antinomian (anti-biblical law) rebels rush headlong into impotence, for, denying that they are under law and law's restraints, they thereby throw away the crucial tool of external conquest and external blessings. They rebel and are destroyed.

---

7. Ethelbert Stauffer, *Christ and the Caesars* (Philadelphia: Westminster Press, 1955).

Conclusion

Men are totally depraved in principle,[8] but not in history. They are in total rebellion in principle, but not in history. There are also depraved comprehensively; everything they are is evil in principle. All their righteousness is as filthy rags (Isa. 64:6). (The Hebrew word for "filthy" is even more graphic.) This is why all men need God's comprehensive redemption.[9]

God definitively heals every aspect of men's lives at the point in time when He regenerates them. He makes them perfect morally *in principle*, but not in history. They are no longer totally depraved in principle; they are perfect men in principle. He heals them completely *in principle*, but not in history. This definitive sanctification then produces the progressive sanctification—setting men apart morally—throughout their lives. Christians work out in history what they are in principle, just as the ethical rebels work out in history what they are in principle.

Neither Christ's perfect humanity in His people nor Satan's total depravity in his people is ever manifested in history. Even Satan's total depravity devel-

---

8. Van Til writes: "For me the idea of total or absolute depravity means that the sinner is *dead* in trespasses and sins (Eph. 2:1). In *principle* man is therefore blind." Van Til, *A Letter on Common Grace*, in *Common Grace and the Gospel*, p. 164.

9. Gary North, "Comprehensive Redemption: A Theology for Social Action," *Journal of Christian Reconstruction*, VIII (Summer 1981).

ops in history.[10] Sin is never overcome fully until the
resurrection at the day of judgment. Similarly, God
restrains the historical outworking of sin in men's
lives until the day of judgment. Then sin-cursed history ends.

Biblical law is both a means of grace (common
and special) and a means of curse (common and special). Men's responses to the terms of biblical law
bring temporal blessings and temporal cursings
(Deut. 28); these responses also bring varying eternal blessings (I Cor. 3:11-15) and varying eternal
cursings (Luke 12:47-48).

The *effects* of covenant-keeping are general in
common grace, and the effects of covenant-breaking
are equally general in common cursing. There are
evil people who get rich in a growing economy, and
there are good people who get killed in losing wars.
But when biblical law restrains evil-doing, all men
are blessed.

History has meaning. The good that evil men do
counts for them eternally, and the evil that righteous
men do counts against them eternally. The basis of

---

10. There is one difficulty here. Satan learns to be more depraved in history. His rejection of God's truth becomes more sinful. Thus, even Satan's total depravity increases. He is a creature; he always has more to learn about God. He always has
more to rebel against, until his ability to rebel is removed at the
day of judgment.

What about Jesus, the perfect human? To what extent does
He learn through history and also in the consummated New
Heavens and New Earth? He said that only the Father knew
when the day judgment would come for Israel (Matt. 24:36). Yet
He and the Father are one (John 10:30). This is a mystery.

meaning in history is judged by the standard of biblical law. Biblical law judges all men and all institutions. All men are held accountable to God. Unredeemed men have the work of the law written in their hearts, while Christians have the law itself written in their hearts.

This is why the cross has meaning in history. It combines common curse and common grace, special curse and special grace. Christ died in order to make history possible — to reduce the historic judgment of God against rebellious mankind. This has benefited covenant-breakers and covenant-keepers alike. Cooperation among men becomes possible by means of Christ's sacrifice. Christ also died to bring eternal life to His people. When God at the end of the millennial age gives up unregenerate people to their lusts, they will revolt against Him, and the final judgment will come.

In summary:

1. Law is a means of grace.
2. Law is the basis of the curses.
3. There are common grace and special grace.
4. There are common curse and special curse.
5. Common grace condemns rebels even more.
6. Evil men do good through God's common grace.
7. God's law is known specially and commonly.

8. External faithfulness to the law brings external blessings.

9. The cross brings salvation to history.

10. The law brings meaning to history.

11. Common grace makes possible human cooperation in history.

12. When God ceases to restrain a covenant-breaking culture, it is destroyed.

3

WHEAT AND TARES: HISTORICAL CONTINUITY

Another parable put he forth unto them, saying, The kingdom of heaven is likened unto a man which sowed good seed in his field. But while men slept, his enemy came and sowed tares among the wheat, and went his way. But when the blade was sprung up, and brought forth fruit, then appeared the tares also. So the servants of the householder came and said unto him, Sir, didst thou not sow good seed in thy field? From whence then hath it tares? He said unto them, An enemy hath done this. The servants said unto him, Wilt thou then that we go and gather them up? But he said, Nay; lest while ye gather up the tares, ye root up also the wheat with them. Let both grow together until the harvest: and in the time of harvest I will say to the reapers, Gather ye together first the tares, and bind them in bundles to burn them: but gather the wheat into my barn (Matt. 13:24-30).

The parable of the wheat and tares is instructive in dealing with the question: Does history reveal a *progressive separation* between the saved and the lost?

The parable begins with the field which is planted
with wheat, but which is sown with tares by an
enemy during the night (Matt. 13:24-30, 36-43).
The parable refers to the building of the kingdom of
God, not simply to the institutional church. "The
field is the world," Christ explained (Matt. 13:37).
The good wheat, the children of God, now must
operate in a world in which the tares, meaning the
unregenerate, are operating. The servants (angels)
instantly recognize the difference, but they are told
not to yank up the tares yet. Such a violent act would
destroy the wheat by plowing up the field. To preserve the growing wheat, the owner allows the tares
to develop. What is preserved is *historical continuity
and development*. Only at the end of the world is a final
separation made. Until then, *for the sake of the wheat*,
the tares are not ripped out.

The parable of the wheat and tares tells us that
the final separation comes at the end of time. Until
then, the two groups must share the same world.
The agricultural parable of wheat and tares implies
slow growth to maturity. We therefore have to conclude that *no radically discontinuous event of separation
will mark the period of historical development*. The total
separation is an event of the last day: the final judgment. It is a discontinuous event that is the capstone
of historical continuity.

The death and resurrection of Christ was probably
the last historically significant event that properly
can be said to be radically discontinuous. (Possibly
the day of Pentecost could serve as the last earth-
shaking, kingdom-shaking event.) The fall of Jerusalem and the destruction of the temple in 70 A.D.

were major discontinuities in history[1], but not on a scale of the death and resurrection of the God-man, Jesus Christ. The next major eschatological discontinuity will be the day of judgment. So we should expect growth in our era, the kind of growth indicated by the agricultural parables.[2]

What must be stressed is the element of *continuous development*. "The kingdom of heaven is like to a grain of mustard seed, which a man took and sowed in his field: Which indeed is the least of all seeds: but when it is grown, it is the greatest among herbs, and becometh a tree, so that the birds of the air come and lodge in the branches thereof" (Matt. 13:31-32). As this kingdom comes into maturity, there is no physical separation between saved and lost. There is, of course, *ethical* separation. Total separation will come only at the end of time. There can be important changes, even as the seasons or changes in familiar weather patterns can speed up or retard growth, but we must not expect a radical separation.

While I do not have the space to demonstrate the point, this means that the *timing* of the separation spoken of by premillennialists—the Rapture—is not in accord with the parables of the kingdom. The Rapture comes at the end of history. The "wheat" cannot be removed from the field until that final day, when we are caught up to meet Christ in the clouds (I Thess. 4:17). There will indeed be a Rapture, but

1. David Chilton, *Days of Vengeance: An Exposition of the Book of Revelation* (Ft. Worth, Texas: Dominion Press, 1986).
2. Gary North, *Moses and Pharaoh: Dominion Religion vs. Power Religion* (Tyler, Texas: Institute for Christian Economics, 1985), ch. 12: "Continuity and Revolution."

it comes at the end of history—when the reapers (angels) harvest the wheat and the tares.

Postmillennialists do not deny the Rapture. It will come on the day of judgment. It will be a post-millennial Rapture. Why a postmillennial Rapture, the amillennialist may say? Why not simply point out that the Rapture comes at the end of time, and let matters drop? The answer is important: we must deal with the question of the historical development of the wheat and tares. We must see that this process of time leads to Christian victory on earth and in time. It leads to victory *in history.* It leads to victory in the *pre-consummation* New Heavens and New Earth (Isa. 65:17-20).

Dominion through Differentiation

An important part of historical development is man's fulfillment of the dominion covenant. New scientific discoveries can be made through the common grace of God, once the care of the field is entrusted to men. The regularities of nature still play a role, but increasingly men devise technologies that substitute for natural processes. In the case of agriculture, for example, fertilizers, irrigation systems, regular care, scientific management, and even satellite surveys are part of the life of the field. Men exercise increasing dominion over the world.

Who Should Rule?

A question then arises: If the devil's followers rule, will they care tenderly for the needs of the godly? Will they exercise dominion for the benefit of the wheat, so to speak? On the other hand, will the tares be cared for by the Christians? If Christians rule, what happens to the unrighteous?

Opponents of biblical law-governed civil rule by Christians often argue that such rule is inherently tyrannical. Unlike the clear message of the Old Testament—that tyranny is the fruit of worshipping false gods, with biblical law as the basis of social peace—we are told that New Testament ethics for some reason requires "neutral" (non-Christian) civil government. Biblical law is somehow tyrannical.[3] Incredibly, most modern Christians believe such humanist propaganda, especially professors who teach in Christian colleges. Too many years studying in humanist graduate school programs have taken their toll. Christian intellectuals have "bought the party line"—the humanist party.

Satan's followers are covenanted to the destroyer. Satan was the original revolutionary and tyrant. He would destroy the wheat if he could. On the other hand, Christians are covenanted to the God who protects the tares from uprooting. Thus, the biblical worldview calls Christians to exercise dominion in the world, not in order to tyrannize non-Christians, but rather to preserve law and order—God's law and God's order, the only kind that the Bible requires. The wheat is required by God to recognize the right of the tares to conduct themselves without interference, except when they publicly violate biblical law.

The Bible acknowledges the freedom of both

---

3. For a Bible-based refutation of such views, see Greg L. Bahnsen, *By This Standard: The Authority of God's Law Today* (Tyler, Texas: Institute for Christian Economics, 1986).

tares and wheat to work out their respective destinies with fear and trembling. This freedom can safely be granted ethical rebels *because of the greater productivity of the righteous*. The wealth of the unrighteous is laid up for the just (Prov. 13:22b). In confidence, *Christians need not fear the peaceful, competitive efforts of our ethical opponents*.

In contrast, our opponents have every reason to fear us — not because we are tyrants, but because the world is structured and governed by God in such a way as to produce historical victory for His law-abiding people. We get richer, wiser, and culturally dominant when we are faithful to God's law (Deut. 28:1-14); our opponents get poorer, more foolish, and culturally irrelevant when they violate the terms of the covenant (Deut. 28:15-68). This disturbs them. They do not want a "fair fight," meaning open competition. They want control by the State and then control over the State. They want power, for they cannot achieve long-term dominion. They worship the power religion.

Too many modern Christians worship in the tabernacles of the escape religion, the other alternative to the dominion religion that is required by the Bible.[4] All they want is to be left alone by the God-haters. The best way to achieve this goal, they erroneously believe, is to avoid confrontation with unbelievers, especially political confrontation. They therefore remove themselves from politics.

They also feel compelled to justify their retreat from responsibility by affirming the existence of a

---

4. Gary North, *Moses and Pharaoh*, Introduction.

supposed God-given right of power-seeking God-haters to impose "neutral" humanist civil law on Christians. These Christians defend humanist civil law in the name of freedom. They say that biblical law in the hands of Christians will *always* lead to tyranny. (But they admit readily that biblical law in the Old Testament, before the resurrection of Christ, and before He sent the Holy Spirit to lead His church into all truth, was the basis of peace and freedom. You figure it out; it is beyond my powers of comprehension.) They are saying implicitly that the tares can be trusted to care for the needs of the field, including the wheat, but the wheat cannot be trusted to care for the field at all.

The fact is, we need biblical law in order to preserve historical continuity. We need biblical law in order to avoid humanism's religion of revolution, especially Marx's version.[5] In order to be preserved, the field (world) needs Christians in positions of authority in every area of life; this means that the reprobates will be treated lawfully. They will be given civil freedom precisely *because* humanists (such as bloody Marxists, bloody Nazis, and bloody Muslims) will *not* be in control.

Differentiation

God intends for the dominion religion of the Bible to triumph over both the power religion and the escape religion. This is the fundamental issue of *differentiation in history.* Men are not passive. They are commanded to be active, to seek dominion over

---

5. Gary North, *Marx's Religion of Revolution: The Doctrine of Creative Destruction* (Nutley, New Jersey: Craig Press, 1968).

nature (Gen. 1:28; 9:1-7). They are to manage the field (world). They are to work out their salvation or damnation in fear and trembling (Phil. 2:12b).

As good people and evil people work out their God-ordained destinies, what kind of development can be expected? Who prospers most, the saved or the lost? Who becomes dominant in history? Christians do. They have the tool of dominion, biblical law, and they have the Holy Spirit.

Do they become dominant only after the Rapture? No, they become dominant before the Rapture. The Rapture takes place simultaneously with the final judgment. Remember, the parable tells us that there will be no premature separation of wheat from tares; that happens only once, at judgment day.

Or will Christians become dominant only after the final judgment, when God establishes the *fully consummated* New Heaven and New Earth? No, they will become dominant before the final judgment, since God has *already* established the New Heavens and the New Earth at Christ's resurrection. This is why Isaiah 65:17-20 speaks of the New Heavens and the New Earth as a place where sinners still operate, indicating a pre-final-judgment kingdom.[6]

How will Christians achieve dominion? By faithful service to God. By what standard are Christians to evaluate faithful service? By biblical law. They are to become earthly judges — self-judges first, and then judges in every area of life.

---

6. David Chilton's *Days of Vengeance* discusses Revelation 21 and 22 in terms of the pre-consummation manifestation of the New Heavens and the New Earth.

Dominion through Superior Judgment

Isaiah 32 is a neglected portion of Scripture in our day. It informs us of a remarkable era that is coming. It is an era of "epistemological self-consciousness," to use Cornelius Van Til's phrase. It is an era when men will know God's standards and apply them accurately to the historical situation. It is not an era beyond the final judgment, for it speaks of churls as well as liberal people. Yet it cannot be an era that is inaugurated by a radical separation between saved and lost (the Rapture), for such a separation comes only at the end of time. This era will come before Christ returns physically to earth in judgment. We read in the first eight verses:

Behold, a king shall reign in righteousness, and princes shall rule in judgment. And a man shall be as an hiding place from the wind, and a covert from the tempest; as rivers of water in a dry place, as the shadow of a great rock in a weary land. And the eyes of them that see shall not be dim, and the ears of them that hear shall hearken. The heart also of the rash shall understand knowledge, and the tongue of the stammerers shall be ready to speak plainly. The vile person shall be no more called liberal, nor the churl said to be bountiful. For the vile person will speak villany, and his heart will work iniquity, to practise hypocrisy, and to utter error against the LORD, to make empty the soul of the hungry, and he will cause the drink of the thirsty to fail. The instruments also of the churl are

evil; he deviseth wicked devices to destroy the
poor with lying words, even when the needy
speaketh right. But the liberal deviseth liberal
things: and by liberal things shall he stand.

To repeat, "The vile person shall be no more
called liberal, nor the churl said to be bountiful" (v.
5). Churls persist in their churlishness; liberal men
continue to be gracious. It does not say that all
churls will be converted, but it also does not say that
the liberals shall be destroyed. The two exist together. But the language of promise indicates that
Isaiah knew full well that in his day (and in our day),
churls are called liberal, and vice versa. Men refuse
to apply their knowledge of God's standards to the
world in which they live. But it shall not always be
thus.

Exercising Biblical Judgment
At this point, we face two crucial questions. The
answers separate many Christian commentators.
First, should we expect this knowledge to come instantaneously? Second, when this prophesied world of epistemological self-consciousness finally dawns, which
group will be the earthly victors, churls or liberals?
The amillennialist must answer that this parallel
development of knowledge is gradual. The postmillenialist agrees. Wheat and tares develop together.
There is *continuity in history.*
The premillennialist (especially the dispensationalist) dissents. The premillennial position is that this
future era of accurate judgment will come only after

the Rapture and the subsequent establishment of an earthly kingdom, with Christ ruling on earth in person. Christians cannot achieve such good judgment apart from perfect redemption and then Christ's physical presence in history. Christians must wait for the physical return of Christ, at which time (1) they will be given perfect judgment, (2) they will be instantaneously wholly regenerated, (3) they will be clothed in perfect, sin-free, eternal, indestructible bodies, and then (4) they will be sent back to rule over the "common sinful folk" who were left behind at the Rapture and who have not been given eternal, sin-free bodies. The ability to exercise accurate judgment is therefore the product of a radical break into (or out of) history.

The amillennial position sees no era of pre-consummation, pre-final-judgment righteousness. Such righteousness will exist only in the church, and the church will come under increasing persecution. Therefore, he concludes that the growth in good judgment does separate the saved from the lost culturally, but since there is no coming era of godly victory culturally, the amillennialist has to say that this ethical and epistemological separation leads to the defeat of Christians on the battlefields of culture. Evil will triumph before the final judgment, and since this process is continuous, *the decline into darkness must be part of the process of differentiation over time*. This increase in righteous judgment on the part of the church nevertheless is overcome culturally by the victory of Satan's forces over the church.

The postmillennialist categorically rejects such a

view of knowledge. As the ability of Christians to make accurate, God-honoring judgments in history increases over time, more authority is transferred to them. Faithfulness to the terms of the covenant brings additional blessings (Deut. 28:1-14). The converse is also true: as men increase in unrighteousness, God's curses overtake them (Deut. 28:15-68). As pagans lose their ability to make such judgments, as a direct result of their denial of and war against biblical law, authority will be removed from them, just as it was removed from Israel in 70 A.D.

Obedient response to true knowledge, in the postmillennial framework, leads to blessing in history, not a curse. It leads to the victory of God's people, not their defeat. But the amillennialist has to deny this. The increase of true self-knowledge that Isaiah 32 predicts becomes a curse for Christians in the amillennial system. Van Til makes this idea fundamental in his book on common grace. We will examine his arguments in chapter 4.

Conclusion

Christ's parable of the wheat and tares emphasizes historical continuity prior to the final judgment. The kingdom of God will not be interrupted by any radical break that separates evil people from righteous people. They mature side by side. Removing the evil people — the suggestion of the servants — would hurt the righteous. This points to the need for social cooperation and the division of labor in history. Men need each other's skills and services in order to work out their earthly destinies. The unrighteous people are protected from destruction in history for the sake of the righteous.

Christians are called by God to take dominion in every area of life. God expects Christians to rule righteously, meaning in terms of His revealed law. If they order their lives and institutions in terms of God's law, they will find that they exercise greater and greater authority. They will not be in earthly bondage to humanists forever. This was the lesson of Joseph in the prison, the three Hebrew youths in Nebuchadnezzar's fiery furnace, Daniel in the lions' den, and Jesus on the cross. In the case of Jesus' death, the worst injustice in history led to His attainment to total cosmic power. "And Jesus came and spake unto them, saying, All power is given to me in heaven and in earth" (Matt. 28:18).

As history progresses, the saved and the lost differentiate themselves ethically. The righteous become dominant, not through the exercise of lawless power, but through obedience to biblical law. A continuous ethical separation takes place over time.

Eventually, men begin to apply God's standards to earthly situations, and they will recognize the difference between churls and righteous people. Liberal (generous) people will devise liberal things, and stand in terms of what they have devised. As men develop their skills in making godly judgments, they will gain greater authority. The satanists will not dominate history through power, nor will Christ and His angels uproot the tares (let alone the wheat) in history before both wheat and tares have fully matured. Thus, neither the amillennial vision nor

the premillennial vision is correct. The church will
not be defeated in history before Christ returns physically to rule. The gates of hell shall not stand
against the offensive onslaught of Christ's church.

In summary:

1. Wheat and tares remain in the field until
the final judgment.

2. The tares (unrighteous) are preserved
for the sake of the wheat (righteous).

3. All men are under the terms of the dominion covenant (Gen. 1:27-28).

4. Satanists would prefer to uproot the
wheat,

5. God tells His followers to leave the tares
alone, so long as they are obedient publicly to
His law.

6. No radical uprooting of the wheat in history is spoken of anywhere in the Bible.

7. No radical uprooting of the tares in history is spoken of in the Bible.

8. The next discontinuous eschatological
event is the final judgment.

9. The Rapture takes place immediately
preceding the final judgment.

10. The separation in time is ethical.

11. Men will eventually identify churls and
generous people accurately.

12. This increase in wisdom takes time; it
does not happen overnight.

13. Authority is steadily captured by Christians because of their greater covenantal faithfulness, better judgment, and greater reliability.

4

VAN TIL'S VERSION
OF COMMON GRACE

*There shall be no more thence an infant of days,
nor an old man that hath not filled his days: for the
child shall die an hundred years old; but the sinner being
an hundred years old shall be accursed (Isa. 65:20).*

Isaiah describes an era of earthly blessing. Its
prime mark is life without death for long periods.
This is the blessing of *personal historical continuity.* No
more deaths for children. Sinners die at age one
hundred, and are accounted accursed. This is clearly
the era before the final judgment, for sinners still live
and die. (There will be no sin or death in the post-
resurrection world.) The common grace of God extends to sinners: long life.

There is no verse in the Bible more devastating
to amillennial eschatology. Amillennialists must alle-
gorize it away, or better yet, ignore it. Isaiah is
speaking here of the New Heavens and New Earth:
"For, behold, I create new heavens and a new earth:

and the former shall not be remembered, nor come to mind" (65:17). There is a manifestation of this era in history. It began with Christ's resurrection, the greatest manifestation of God's kingdom, and it develops throughout New Testament history. This is the biblical basis for the idea of progress, a uniquely Christian idea: an eschatology of victory in history over the physical effects of sin, meaning victory in history over God's curse. I cannot stress this too much: *victory in history.*

Continuity: Common Grace

We now return to the question of common grace. I have already defined common grace as continuity (Introduction). The question now presents itself: What is the nature of this continuity?

Withdrawing Common Grace: Amillennialism

The amillennialist says that the slow, downward drift of culture parallels the growth in self-awareness and improving judgment. This has to mean that *common grace is to be withdrawn as time progresses.* The restraining hand of God will be progressively removed. Since the amillennialist believes that things will get worse before the final judgment, he has to interpret common grace as *earlier* grace (assuming he admits the existence of common grace at all). This has been stated most forcefully by Van Til, who holds a doctrine of common grace and who is a self-conscious amillennialist:

All common grace is earlier grace. Its commonness lies in its earliness. It pertains not merely to the lower dimensions of life. It pertains to all dimensions of life, but to all these dimensions ever decreasingly as the time of history goes on. At the very first stage of history there is much common grace. There is a common good nature under the common favor of God. But this creation-grace requires response. It cannot remain what it is. It is conditional. Differentiation must set in and does set in. It comes first in the form of a common rejection of God. Yet common grace continues; it is on a "lower" level now; it is long-suffering that men may be led to repentance. God still continues to present Himself for what He is, both in nature and in the work of redemption. The differentiation meanwhile proceeds. . . . Common grace will diminish still more in the further course of history. With every conditional act the remaining significance of the conditional is reduced. God allows men to follow the path of their self-chosen rejection of Him more rapidly than ever toward the final consummation. God increases His attitude of wrath upon the reprobate as time goes on, until at the end of time, at the great consummation of history, their condition has caught up with their state.[1]

Because all men's self-knowledge increases over

1. Van Til, *Common Grace*, in *Common Grace and the Gospel*, pp. 82-83.

time, the reprobate man's self-knowledge therefore increases. Self-knowledge is a good thing, a gift from God. Romans 7 teaches that the increase in self-knowledge that biblical law brings can produce in men a sense of death, which through God's grace leads to life. I should think that we would associate such an increase in the self-knowledge of the reprobate with an increase of common grace. Yet Van Til says the opposite: it leads to a reduction of common grace. This is an oddity of his exposition. There is a reason for it: his amillennial eschatology.

He says also that "God allows men to follow the path of their self-chosen rejection of Him more rapidly than ever toward the final consummation. God increases His attitude of wrath upon the reprobate as time goes on, until at the end of time, at the great consummation of history, their condition has caught up with their state." But be forewarned: he also argues (as we shall see) that the reprobate will progressively triumph over the church in history. Thus, Van Til is arguing implicitly that *God's increasing wrath to the unregenerate leads to their increasing external victory over the church in history*. God says, in effect, "I hate you so much, and My hatred is increasing so rapidly, that I will let you kick the stuffing out of My people, whom I love with an increasing fervor as they increase in righteous self-knowledge." The ways of God are strange . . . if you are an amillennialist.

The condition of the reprobate is one of increasing victory; then, overnight, it turns into total defeat at the final judgment. Yet Van Til describes this *dis-*

continuity as demonstrating continuity: "their condition has caught up with their state." Caught up, indeed—like a speeding truck hitting a pedestrian in a crosswalk, or the crash of a plane carrying home the newly crowned world champion soccer team.

Increasing Common Grace: Postmillennialism

I agree with him that the discontinuity comes after a long continuity. This is the essence of common grace: it increases for generations, and then it is removed overnight. Jesus described the coming judgment of Israel—not, in the postmillennial scheme, the final judgment[2]—in terms of that great discontinuity, Noah's flood.

> But as the days of Noe were, so shall also the coming of the Son of man be. For as in the days that were before the flood they were eating and drinking, marrying and giving in marriage, until the day that Noe entered into the ark. And [they] knew not until the flood came, and took them all away; so shall the coming of the Son of man be (Matt. 24:37-39).

The pre-flood people had assumed that "business as usual" would continue. Lifespans kept getting longer. The signs of God's grace were everywhere. Then, overnight, it all ended. The greatest extension

---

2. David Chilton, *Paradise Restored: A Biblical Theology of Dominion* (Tyler, Texas: Reconstruction Press, 1985), ch. 11; J. Marcellus Kik, *An Eschatology of Victory* (Nutley, New Jersey: Craig Press, 1971), Section 2.

of common grace in history became the worst disaster in world history. It took the special grace (yet also common grace) of the ark to keep history going.

Van Til's view has common grace receding, and then the judgment hits. This is not what the Bible presents concerning common grace in history. Both common grace and special grace to Noah increased, but only common grace increased for unbelievers. God had Noah construct an ark that would allow God to remove Noah from the midst of the unrighteous. When it was completed, God utterly removed common grace from the world outside the ark. Not only the crumbs falling from God's table were removed, the table itself fell on top of them. Or to put it more precisely, the water table rose to cover them. They were baptized: first by sprinkling, and then by immersion.

Van Til sees continuity in the form of a progressive removal of common grace, with the final judgment culminating this steady continual process. He specifically says that the judgment is the catching up to them of their previous spiritually declining condition. (But how did they get the power to oppress Christians, if God's common grace was being removed from history?) The discontinuity of judgment is, in Van Til's scheme, really simply the culmination of a long process of declining common grace. Then why should any reprobate be surprised when judgment finally comes? Those in Noah's day certainly were.

What the Bible teaches is a different kind of continuity for the unregenerate: a steady increase in common grace as a prelude to the discontinuity of massive judgment.

The Threat of History

Van Til affirms the reality of history, yet it is the history of *continuous ethical decline*. The unregenerate become increasingly powerful as common grace declines. But why? Why should the epistemological self-awareness described in Isaiah 32 necessarily lead to defeat for Christians? What happens to the era of righteousness described in detail in Isaiah 2 and 4:3-5?

By holding to a doctrine of common grace which involves the idea of the common favor of God toward all creatures (except Satan), Van Til then argues that God progressively withdraws this common favor, leaving the unregenerate a free hand to attack God's elect. If common grace is linked with God's favor, and God's favor steadily declines, then that other aspect of common grace, namely, God's restraint, must also be withdrawn. Furthermore, the third feature of common grace, civic righteousness, must also disappear. Van Til does not hesitate to affirm this scenario:

> But when all the reprobate are epistemologically self-conscious, the crack of doom has come. The fully self-conscious reprobate will do all he can in every dimension to destroy the people of God. So while we seek with all our power to hasten the process of differentiation in every dimension we are yet thankful, on the other hand, for "the day of grace," the day of undeveloped differentiation. Such tolerance as we receive on the part of the world is due to this

fact that we live in the earlier, rather than in the later, stage of history. And such influence on the public situation as we can effect, whether in society or in state, presupposes this undifferentiated stage of development.[3]

Consider the implications of what Van Til is saying. *History is an earthly threat to Christian man.* Why? Van Til's amillennial-based argument is that common grace is earlier grace. Common grace declines over time. Why? Because God's attitude of favor declines over time with respect to the unregenerate. With the decline of God's favor, the other benefits of common grace are lost. Evil men become more thoroughly evil.

Then how can they win in history? If common grace gives them law, knowledge, power, and life, and God steadily removes common grace from them, how are they able to win?

This incredibly simple question never appeared in print until I published my original essay in late 1976. As far as I know, no one before my essay ever asked any defender of the common grace doctrine this obvious question. This gives you some indication of how people's eschatological presuppositions blind them to the obvious. The reason why nobody asked the question is that until the 1960's, there were virtually no postmillennialists around who had even read the literature on common grace, and the only one who had, R. J. Rushdoony, did not spot the

---

3. Van Til, *Common Grace*, in *Common Grace and the Gospel*, p. 85.

problem. What seems obvious to a postmillennialist is not obvious to the amillennialist. Meredith Kline read my original essay (as we shall see shortly) and did not even perceive its thesis. He got its argument exactly backwards.

Van Til's argument is the generally accepted one in Reformed circles. His is the standard statement of the common grace position. Yet as the reader should grasp by now, it is deeply flawed. It begins with *false assumptions*: (1) that common grace implies common favor; (2) that this common grace-favor is reduced over time; (3) that this loss of favor necessarily tears down the foundations of civic righteousness within the general culture; (4) that the amillennial vision of the future is accurate. Thus, he concludes that the process of differentiation is leading to the impotence of Christians in every sphere of life, and that we can be thankful for having lived in the period of "earlier" grace, meaning greater common grace.[4]

Multiplying the Confusion

Van Til's view of common grace as prior grace is implicitly opposed to the postmillennialism of R. J.

---

4. In the late 1960's, I wrote to Van Til and asked him how he could reconcile his view of the decline of common grace with his colleague John Murray's postmillennial interpretation of Romans 11. He wrote back and told me he hadn't really thought about it. Since he never subsequently commented on the problem in print, and since he never wrote me a letter clarifying his position, I can only assume that (1) he thought Murray was wrong, but did not want to say so in print, or (2) he thought the question was irrelevant, or (3) he just never thought about it again. I suspect the third explanation is the most likely one.

Rushdoony, yet his view is equally opposed to the amillennialism of the anti-Chalcedon amillennial theologian (and former colleague of Van Til's), Meredith G. Kline, who openly rejects Rushdoony's postmillennial eschatology.

Kline explicitly rejects Van Til's conclusion that common grace declines over time, although he does not mention Van Til as the source of this view. Kline judiciously pins the tail on another donkey. He says that this view of common grace as earlier grace is what the Chalcedon postmillennialists teach. Kline is incorrect: Greg Bahnsen, James Jordan, David Chilton, and I all reject this view of common grace, and we are all Chalcedon-trained postmillennialists. We were all on the payroll of Chalcedon in the 1970's. (And one by one, we all left Chalcedon as we came to it: fired with enthusiasm!) The original essay from which this book is derived appeared in *The Journal of Christian Reconstruction* two years before Kline's essay was published, and which he cites, clearly not having understood it. Only R. J. Rushdoony has affirmed Van Til's view of common grace, despite the fact that such a view conflicts with his postmillennialism.[5]

---

5. Rushdoony categorically rejects amillennialism, calling it "impotent religion" and "blasphemy" — an implicit attack on Van Til — yet he affirms the validity of Van Til's common grace position, calling for the substitution of Van Til's "earlier grace" concept for "common grace." Rushdoony's anti-amillennial essay appeared in *Journal of Christian Reconstruction*, III (Winter 1976-77): "Postmillennialism versus Impotent Religion." His pro-"earlier grace" statement appeared in his review of E. L. Hebden Taylor's book, *The Christian Philosophy of Law, Politics and the State*,

Kline rejects postmillennialism, especially the biblical law variety, and this is what led to his complete misreading of the postmillennial view of common grace. He thought he was attacking theonomic postmillennialism, when he was in fact attacking Van Til. By rejecting the idea that common grace declines over time, Kline breaks radically with Van Til. It is unlikely that Kline even recognizes the anti-Van Til implications of what he has written, any more than Rushdoony has recognized the anti-postmillennial implications of Van Til's position on common grace. In his own intellectual reputation-ruining review essay of Greg Bahnsen's *Theonomy in Christian Ethics*, Kline writes:

---

in *Westminster Theological Journal*, XXX (Nov. 1967): "A concept of 'earlier grace' makes remnants of justice, right, and community tenable; a concept of 'common grace' does not" (p. 100). "The term 'common grace' has become a shibboleth of Dutch theology and a passageway across the Jordan and into Reformed territory of those who can feign the required accent. Has not the time come to drop the whole concept and start afresh?" (p. 101).

This was the last essay for the *Westminster Theological Journal* that Rushdoony was ever invited to submit. Despite its well-deserved reputation for publishing lengthy reviews of books by some of the most obscure liberal European theologians, this Calvinistic journal has enforced a quarter-century blackout on reviews of Rushdoony's books, with the one exception of John Frame's review of *Institutes of Biblical Law*, which Frame, as a faculty member at Westminster, pressured the *Journal* to publish. Apparently the editors believe that reviews of books by the most wide-ranging and influential Reformed scholar of the second half of the twentieth century are inappropriate. Refuting obscure German liberals—that's what makes a difference for the kingdom of God!

Along with the hermeneutical deficiencies of Chalcedon's millennialism there is a fundamental theological problem that besets it. And here we come around again to Chalcedon's confounding the biblical concepts of the holy and the common. As we have seen, Chalcedon's brand of postmillennialism envisages as the climax of the millennium something more than a high degree of success in the church's evangelistic mission to the world. An additional millennial prospect (one which they particularly relish) is that of a material prosperity and a world-wide eminence and dominance of Christ's established kingdom on earth, with a divinely enforced submission of the nations to the world government of the Christocracy. . . . The insuperable theological objection to any and every such chiliastic construction is that it entails the assumption of a premature eclipse of the order of common grace. . . . In thus postulating the termination of the common grace order before the consummation, Chalcedon's postmillennialism in effect attributes unfaithfulness to God, for God committed himself in his ancient covenant to maintain that order for as long as the earth endures.[6]

It is not Chalcedon's postmillennialists who predict the erosion of the common grace order, but

---

6. Meredith G. Kline, "Comments on an Old-New Error," *Westminster Theological Journal*, XLI (Fall 1978), pp. 183, 184.

rather Van Til. "Common grace will diminish still more in the further course of history."[7] It is he who says that common grace is prior grace. "All common grace is earlier grace."[8] The postmillennialist position is that common grace is essentially future grace. As I wrote in my original essay, which Kline's footnotes indicate that he read, but whose summary indicates that he obviously did no read carefully: "Therefore *common grace* is essentially *future grace*."[9] Again, *"Common grace has not yet fully developed."*[10] My emphases were in the original essay. I wanted even the laziest and most ill-equipped reader to understand my point. Dr. Kline did not understand my point.

(This time, to help Dr. Kline understand what I am trying to say, I have added one-sentence, numbered summaries at the end of each chapter. This kills two birds with one stone. People keep telling Christian Reconstructionist writers that we write books that are too difficult. We need to simplify our books, they tell us. We need to write for the average reader without any theological background. Well, I have gone the extra mile. I have written it so that even Dr. Kline can understand it.)

The postmillennialist argues that things will improve over time. Anyway, most things will improve

---

7. *Common Grace*, in *Common Grace and the Gospel*, p. 83.

8. *Ibid.*, p. 82.

9. Gary North, "Common Grace, Eschatology, and Biblical Law," *Journal of Christian Reconstruction*, III (Winter 1976-77), p. 45.

10. *Ibid.*, p. 41.

over time. An increase of special grace (more bread on the table of the faithful) leads to more common grace (crumbs under the table). Common grace is not earlier grace; it is later grace.

Van Til rejects such a view. Neither Kline nor Rushdoony recognizes the extent to which Van Til's amillennialism has colored and distorted his whole doctrine of common grace. Perhaps unconsciously, he selectively structured the biblical evidence on this question in order to make it conform with his Netherlands amillennial heritage. This is why his entire concept of common grace is incorrect: his eschatology is incorrect.

It is imperative that Christians scrap the concept of "earlier grace" and adopt a doctrine of common (crumbs for the dogs) grace. As special grace increases, so will common grace. As the world gets richer and more peaceful, the "dogs" benefit.

The amazing irony of all this is that Rushdoony never recognized the threat to his postmillennialism that Van Til's view of common grace presents. He therefore never attempted to explain how postmillennialism and Van Til's common grace doctrine can be reconciled. Obviously, they cannot be reconciled. They are opposites. Nevertheless, Rushdoony's infrequent and undeveloped references to common grace indicate that this doctrine has not been very important in his thinking, and the contradiction between Van Til's common grace doctrine and postmillennialism was a loose end that Rushdoony, in his enormous output of books and essays, unfortunately overlooked. Yet Kline, in his rush to condemn what he thought was Chalcedon's postmillennialism, mistook Rushdoony's view of common grace as the postmillennial view, despite the fact that on this question, Rushdoony has adopted the amillennial viewpoint. Kline therefore attacked Van Til's view indirectly by attacking Rushdoony directly. Confusion was multiplied on all sides.

A Postmillennial Response

In response to Van Til, I offer three criticisms. First, God does not favor the unregenerate at any time after the rebellion of man. Man is totally depraved, and there is nothing in him deserving praise or favor, nor does God look favorably on him. God grants the unregenerate man favors (not favor) in order to heap coals of fire on his head (if he is not part of the elect) or else to call him to repentance (which God's special grace accomplishes). Thus, God is hostile to the ethical rebel throughout history and eternity. God hates unregenerate men with a perfect hatred from beginning to end, for they are totally depraved from beginning to end. "Earlier" has nothing to do with it. On this point, the Protestant Reformed Church is correct.

Second, once the excess theological baggage of God's supposed favor toward the unregenerate is removed, the other two issues can be discussed: God's restraining of apostate man, and apostate man's civic righteousness.

Biblical Law and Restraint

The activity of God's Spirit is important in understanding the nature of God's restraint, but we are told virtually nothing of the operation of the Spirit. What we *are* told is that *the law of God restrains men.* They do the work of the law written on their hearts (Rom. 2:14-15). This law is the primary means of God's external blessings (Deut. 28:1-14); rebellion against His law brings destruction (Deut. 28:15-68). Therefore, as the reign of biblical law is extended by means of the preaching of the whole counsel of God, and as the law is written in the hearts of regenerate men (Jer. 31:33-34; Heb. 8:10-11; 10:16), and as the unregenerate come under the sway and influence of the law, common grace must *increase*, not decrease. The central issue is the restraint by God inherent in the work of the law. This work is in every man's heart.

Remember, this has nothing to do with the supposed favor of God toward mankind in general. It is simply that as Christians become more faithful to biblical law, they receive more bread from the hand of God. As they increase the amount of bread on their tables, more crumbs fall to the "dogs" beneath. Common grace increases as special grace increases.

Biblical Law and Civic Righteousness

The amillennial view of the process of separation or differentiation is seriously flawed by a lack of understanding of the power which biblical law confers on those who seek to abide by its standards. Again, we must look at Deuteronomy, chapter eight. Conformity to the precepts of the law brings external blessings, but these blessings can (though they need not) serve as a snare and a temptation, for men may forget the source of their blessings. Men can forget God, claim autonomy, and turn away from the law. This leads to their destruction. The formerly faithful people are scattered.

Thus, we see the paradox of Deuteronomy 8. First, covenantal faithfulness to biblical law produces external blessings by God in response to men's faithfulness. Second, God's blessings lead to the temptation of relying on the blessings as if they were the product of man's hands. Third, this temptation, if men fall into it, then brings judgment. The blessings can therefore sometimes lead to disaster and impotence. This is the paradox. Conclusion: *long-term adherence to the terms of biblical law is basic for external long-term success*. Short-term adherence leads to the judgment of God in history—or at the end of time, destroying history.

The unregenerate have the work of the law in their hearts (Rom. 2:14-15). This does not lead them to repent, but it offers them a tool of earthly dominion. If they abide by what their consciences tell them, they can prosper. They hate God, but they love wealth. For a time, their love of the external blessings can overcome their hatred of God and the concomitant love of death (Prov. 8:36b). Furthermore, in times of increasing special grace, Christians will also obey God's law. The principles of biblical law become common practice. External covenant blessings become widespread. It is in these periods of increasing external blessings in response to men's external obedience that biblical law can produce civil righteousness among the unregenerate.

Dominion through Ethics

As men become epistemologically self-conscious, they must face up to reality — God's reality. Ours is a moral universe. It is governed by a law-order which reflects the moral character of God. When men finally realize who the churls are and who the liberals are, they have made a significant discovery. They recognize the relationship between God's standards and the ethical decisions of men. In short, they come to grips with the law of God. The *law* is written in the hearts of Christians (Heb. 8:10-11; 10:16). The *work of the law* is written in the hearts of all men (Rom. 2:14-15). The Christians are therefore increasingly in touch with the source of *legitimate* earthly power: biblical law.

Van Til has emphasized the importance of the distinction between the covenantal law which *in principle* is written on the hearts of Christians (Heb. 8:9-13) and the *work* of the law which is in the hearts of unregenerate people (Rom. 2:14-15). They are not the same form of heart-written law. Commenting on Romans 2:14-15, he writes:

> It is true that they have the law written in their hearts. Their own make-up as image-bearers of God tells them, as it were, in the imperative voice, that they must act as such. All of God's revelation to man is law to man. But here we deal with man's response as an ethical being to this revelation of God. All men, says Paul, to some extent, do the works of the law. He says that they have the *works* of the law writ-

ten in their hearts. Without a true motive,
without a true purpose, they may still do that
which externally appears as acts of obedience to
God's law. God continues to press his demands
upon man, and man is good "after a fashion"
just as he knows "after a fashion."[11]

What I want to point out is Van Til's understanding of the possibility of unregenerate men's *external conformity* to the *external requirements* of biblical
law. Unregenerate men can obey the law externally
"after a fashion." This is a very important insight for
developing a proper understanding of common
grace. (Sadly, Van Til failed to develop it.) They do
what is right for the wrong motive. But any right external action counts for something, temporally and
eternally. Better to be an Albert Schweitzer, on earth
or in hell, than an Adolph Hitler.

Adherence to biblical law brings external rewards, including legitimate temporal power (Deut.
28:7, 13). To match the God-ordained legitimate
power of *covenantally faithful* Christians, the unregenerate must conform their actions externally to the law
of God as preached by Christians, the work of which
they already have in their hearts. The unregenerate
are therefore made far more responsible before God,
simply because they have more knowledge. They de-
sire power. Christians will some day possess cultural, economic, and political power through their

---

11. Van Til, *An Introduction to Systematic Theology*, Vol. V of *In
Defense of the Faith*, p. 105.

adherence to biblical law. Therefore, in order to compete with the righteous, unregenerate men will have to imitate special covenantal faithfulness by adhering to the external demands of God's covenants.

The unregenerate will at last bring down the final wrath of God upon their heads—the crack of doom—because of their rebellious misuse of the *external power* they have gained in response to their increased conformity to the *external requirements* of biblical law. At the end of time, they revolt. They revolt against God and His common grace. They revolt against a greater manifestation in history of His common grace, for *common grace is future grace*. They also revolt with a greater measure of God-given power. Because of their greater knowledge of the truth, their judgment is that much more severe. From him to whom much is given, much is expected (Luke 12:47-48).

The unregenerate have only two unregenerate choices: either conform themselves to biblical law (or at least to the work of the law written on their hearts), or, second, abandon biblical law and thereby abandon dominion. They can gain long-term power only on God's terms: acknowledgement of and conformity to God's law. There is no other way. Any turning from biblical law eventually brings impotence, fragmentation, and despair. Furthermore, it leaves those with a commitment to biblical law in the driver's seat. Increasing differentiation over time, therefore, does not lead to the progressive impotence of the Christians. It leads to their victory culturally. They see the implications of the law more clearly. So do their enemies. The unrighteous can gain access to the blessings only by accepting God's moral universe as it is. The creation itself testifies to the holiness of God. They must sit under God's table.

The Hebrews were told to separate themselves from the people and the gods of the land. Those gods were the gods of Satan, the gods of chaos, moral dissolution, and cyclical history. The pagan world was faithful to the doctrine of cycles: there can be no straight-line progress. But the Hebrews were told differently. If they were faithful, God said, they would not suffer the burdens of sickness, and no one and no animal would suffer miscarriages (Ex. 23:24-26). Special grace leads to a commitment to the law; the commitment to God's law permits God to reduce the common curse element of nature's law, leaving proportionately more common grace—the reign of *beneficent common law.*

The curse of nature can therefore be steadily reduced, but only if men conform themselves to revealed law or to the work of the law in their hearts. One important visible blessing then comes in the form of a more productive, less scarcity-dominated nature. There can be *positive feedback* in the relation between law and blessing: the blessings will confirm God's faithfulness to His law, which in turn will lead to greater convenantal faithfulness (Deut. 8:18). This is the answer to the paradox of Deuteronomy 8: man's ethical history need not become a cyclical spiral. Of course, special grace is required to keep a people faithful in the long run. Without special grace, the temptation to forget the source of wealth takes over, and the end result is destruction. This is why, at the end of the millennial age, the unregener-ate try once again to assert their autonomy from God. They attack the church of the faithful (Rev. 20:8-9a). They attempt once more to exercise auton-omous power. And the crack of doom sounds, not for the regenerate (for which there is no doom), but rather for the unregenerate (Rev. 20:9b).

Differentiation and Progress

The process of differentiation is not constant over time. It ebbs and flows. Its general direction is to-ward epistemological self-consciousness. But Chris-tians are not always faithful, any more than the He-brews were in the days of the judges. The early church defeated pagan Rome, but then the secular remnants of Rome compromised the church. The Reformation launched a new era of cultural growth, but the Counter-Reformation struck back, and the secularism of the Renaissance and then the Enlight-enment overshadowed both, and still does.

This is not cyclical history, for history is linear. There was a creation, a Fall, a people called out of bondage, an incarnation, a resurrection, and Pente-cost. There will be an era of epistemological self-consciousness, as promised in Isaiah 32. There will be a final rebellion and judgment. There has been a Christian nation called the United States. There has been a secular nation called the United States. (The dividing line was the Civil War, or War of Southern Secession, or War Between the States, or War of Northern Aggression—take your pick.) Back and forth, ebb and flow, but with a long-range goal. History is headed somewhere.

There has also been progress. We see this especially in the progress of Christian creeds. Look at the Apostles' Creed. Then look at the Westminster Confession of Faith. Only a fool or a heretic would deny theological progress. There has also been a parallel growth in wealth, knowledge, and culture. Are the two developments, theological and cultural, completely unrelated? What are we to say, that technology as such is the devil's, and that since God's common grace has supposedly been steadily withdrawn as the creeds have been steadily improved, the modern world's development is therefore the autonomous creative work of Satan (since God's common grace cannot account for this progress)? Is Satan creative —autonomously creative? If not, from whence comes our wealth, our knowledge, and our power? Is it not from God? Is not Satan the great imitator? But whose progress has he imitated? Whose cultural development has he attempted to steal, twist, and destroy? Where did the progress come from—and how?

There has been progress since the days of Noah —not straight-line progress, not pure compound growth, but progress nonetheless. Christianity produced it, secularism stole it, and today we seem to be at another crossroad: Can the Christians sustain what they began, given their present compromises with secularism? Can the secularists sustain what they and the Christians have constructed, now that their spiritual capital is running low, and the Christians' cultural bank account is close to empty?

Escape-oriented Christians and power-seeking secularists today are, in the field of education and other "secular" realms, like a pair of drunks who lean on each other in order not to fall down. Using Deuteronomy 8 as a model, we seem to be in the "blessings unto temptation" (8:17) stage, with "rebellion unto destruction" (8:19-20) looming ahead. If nothing else, AIDS is a good indication of God's displeasure. Judgment has happened before; it can happen again. In this sense, it is the *lack* of Christians' epistemological self-consciousness in our day that seems to be responsible for the *reduction* of common grace. Yet it is Van Til's view that the increase of epistemological self-consciousness is responsible for, or at least parallels, the reduction of common grace. Amillennialism has crippled his analysis of common grace. So has his equation of God's gifts and God's supposed favor to mankind in general.

The separation between the wheat and the tares is progressive. It is not a straight-line progression. Floods and droughts hit wheat and tares in turn. Sometimes they hit both at once. Sometimes the sun and rain help both to grow at the same time. But there is maturity. The tares grow unto final destruction, and the wheat grows unto final blessing. In the meantime, both have roles to play in God's plan for the ages. At least the tares help keep the soil from eroding. Better tares than the destruction of the field, at least for the present. They serve God, despite themselves. There has been progress for both wheat and tares. Greek and Roman science became static; Christian concepts of optimism and an or-

derly universe created modern science.[12] Now the
tares run the scientific world, but for how long? Until a nuclear war? Until the concepts of meaningless
Darwinian evolution and modern indeterminate
physics destroy the concept of regular law—the
foundation of all science?

How long can we go on like this? Answer: until
epistemological self-consciousness brings Christians
back to the law of God. Then the pagans must imitate them or quit. Obedience to God alone brings
long-term dominion.

Primacy: Epistemology or Ethics?

In Van Til's view, history is a threat to the church
of Jesus Christ. Common grace is prior grace; as
men's knowledge of themselves, their presuppositions, and their futures increases, the church gets
weaker, and the satanists get stronger. An increase in
knowledge is therefore a threat to the church.

The reason why Van Til's *Common Grace and the
Gospel* is so difficult to read, and so muddled in its exposition, is that Van Til's preference for asking questions about epistemology ruined his insights concerning common grace and history. He spends the
whole book asking the wrong questions. He keeps
asking questions about continuity and discontinuity,
not in terms of history (eschatology) and ethics (biblical law), but in terms of *epistemology*. He keeps

---

12. Stanley Jaki, *The Road of Science and the Ways to God* (University of Chicago Press, 1978); *Science and Creation: From eternal
cycles to an oscillating universe* (Edinburgh and London: Scottish
Academic Press, [1974] 1980).

bringing up the question of the continuity/discontinuity problems of the human mind: God to mankind in general, reprobate to reprobate, and reprobate to redeemed. The problem with this approach is twofold: (1) his membership in the Christian Reformed Church led him to accept the Synod's 1924 statement that common grace implies the favor of God toward the unregenerate, and (2) his amillennial eschatology led him to conclude that common grace declines over time.

His whole theology rests on his argument that *the fundamental issues of life are ethical, not intellectual*. But he cannot explain the historical reality of the greater and greater external cooperation of unbelievers and believers over time—a cooperation that has produced Western civilization's historically unprecedented growth in every area of life. Common grace is obviously increasing, yet he has to say that it is steadily decreasing. Why? Because he says that increasing *epistemological* self-consciousness necessarily leads to increasing *ethical* self-consciousness, which means that reprobates will grow more evil. This means that God must show less favor to them over time. This means a reduction in common grace. The problem for Van Til's exposition is this: God shows greater common grace to them over time. They keep getting richer and more powerful. How can this be?

I answer in response to Van Til that their increase in epistemological self-consciousness does not lead to an increase in ethical self-consciousness, at least not in the sense that their increasing knowledge of God's orderly world leads them to act in terms of their intellectual belief in Satan's alternative: chaos. They act inconsistently with what they believe. This is one aspect of God's common grace to them: He restrains them from acting consistently with what they officially believe intellectually. They become *more evil* in history because they act *less consistently* with their *intellectual* presuppositions. But ethics is primary, not logic. They gain power because of what they do, not because of what they officially believe.

As the unbelievers grow more *epistemologically* self-conscious, they do *not* grow more *ethically* self-conscious. Instead, they tend to adopt the slogan of Hell Fire Club member Ben Franklin: honesty is the best policy. They also do not commit suicide, which is the ethical end of the truth that all those who hate God love death (Prov. 8:36b).

Here is my thesis: the reprobates' increasing epistemological self-consciousness is not matched by their increasing ethical self-consciousness. Why not? *Because God's common grace restrains this increase in rebellious man's consistency between epistemology and ethics.* His common grace to them increases, but their consistency does not — until the last day, of course.

On the other hand, the Christians' increasing epistemological self-consciousness *is* matched by their increasing ethical self-consciousness. They can *act* consistently with what they *know* to be true about God, man, law, and time. This is why we will win and they will lose in history. We can be consistent and thereby exercise dominion; they cannot be consistent and still gain and retain power.

Van Til's amillennialism, as well as his equating

of common grace and God's favor, led him to reject the most fundamental thesis of his whole academic career: *the primacy of the ethical*. He focused almost all of his attention on the epistemological issues relating to continuity and discontinuity when discussing common grace, rather than focusing on the eschatological and ethical issues.

I want to make my case against Van Til's view of common grace as clear as I can. I am arguing that Van Til confused the fundamental category of common grace—historic continuity—with a philosophical category, epistemological continuity ("What does man know, and how can he know it?"). He devoted his common grace book to the problem of knowledge in history and God's judgment rather than the problem of ethics in history and God's judgment. He ignored biblical law. He was long on Plato and short on Moses. He took the Socratic heresy of salvation by knowledge—"If a man knows the good, he will do the good"—and reversed it to mean reprobation by knowledge: "If he knows the evil, he will do the evil." Here is how he argued:

1. Common grace implies the favor of God to the unregenerate.

2. All men become more epistemologically self-conscious over time (meaning such things as God, man, law, and time).

3. [Implied but never stated] Epistemological self-consciousness logically involves ethical self-consciousness.

4. Both Christians and reprobates will act

out (ethics) their increasing epistemological differences.

5. Evil men will become (act) even more evil.

6. The favor of God will be withdrawn from them over time.

7. They will nevertheless increase in power.

8. They will use this power to persecute Christians.

9. Christians will therefore come under progressive judgment by the reprobate.

10. God will intervene at the end of time to save His nearly defeated church.

All this assumes the validity of amillennial eschatology, though Van Til never mentions that this is the eschatological presupposition of his entire discussion.

As a postmillennialist and a theonomist, I respond to Van Til's position as follows:

1. Common grace does not imply the favor of God to the unregenerate. God in no way favors the unregenerate.

2. All men become more epistemologically self-conscious over time (meaning such things as God, man, law, and time). (Here I agree with Van Til.)

3. Epistemological self-consciousness logically involves ethical self-consciousness. (Logically, yes; historically, no.)

4. God in His granting of common grace *restrains this consistency* in the lives of the unregenerate.

5. Only Christians can act increasingly self-consistent with their epistemological presuppositions and still increase in the blessings of God.

6. Evil men will become (act) even more evil. (Here I agree with Van Til.)

7. To exercise maximum evil, they must act to some extent consistently with the Bible's view of man, time, and law.

8. The favor of God will not be withdrawn from them over time. They never had any favor after Adam's fall. The favor of God has nothing to do with their situation.

9. They will increase in power only when they act in conformity to much of external biblical law (the terms of the covenant).

10. They will attempt to use this power to persecute Christians. (Here I agree with Van Til.)

11. As in the case of the Pharaoh of the exodus and Sodom, this will bring them under the visible judgment of God.

12. Christians will therefore *not* come under progressive judgment by the reprobate; pagan rule will be cut short a "millennium" (a long period of time) before the final judgment.

13. At the end of time, Satan will act consistently with his ethics, but using the power God grants to him. He will therefore act inconsistently with his factual knowledge (as he did when he moved men to crucify Jesus Christ).

14. He will try to destroy the church.

15. God will intervene at the end of time to save His *briefly threatened* church.

Conclusion

Van Til is the major proponent of the common grace doctrine in this century. He has constructed his interpretation of the doctrine on the foundation of an amillennial eschatology. He sees no earthly hope for the church. He sees nothing except cultural, institutional defeat ahead. He begins with this as his operating presupposition, and then constructs his common grace doctrine in terms of it. This is what all other Dutch theologians do, too. The Dutch Reformed theological tradition for two hundred years has been exclusively pessimistic regarding the culture-renovating efforts of God's people. They tell Christians to get busy with the cultural mandate, and they also tell them failure is inevitable. The effects of sin are supposedly too strong.

Such an outlook has led, predictably, to an enclave view of the church and Christian culture, a kind of holding action against the unbeatable satanic enemy. It is not surprising that Christian Reformed Church theologian (and president of Westminster Seminary) R. B. Kuiper warned his fellow Dutch-Americans: "By this time it has become trite to say that we must come out of our isolation. . . . Far too often, let it be said again, we hide our light under a bushel instead of placing it high on a candlestick. We seem not to realize fully that as the salt of the earth we can perform our functions of seasoning and preserving only through contact."[13] But nothing changed,

---

13. R. B. Kuiper, *To Be or Not to Be Reformed: Whither the Christian Reformed Church?* (Grand Rapids, Michigan, Zondervan, 1959), p. 186.

except that the leadership of the church has grown more liberal than it was in Kuiper's day. The Christian Reformed Church still speaks with a Dutch accent. So does the Protestant Reformed Church.

People who do not believe that the Christian civilization will ever become a city on a hill, and a light to the nations, and who recognize that there are extreme risks in trying to build such a city, are unlikely to accept those risks. Why bother? It is safer to keep your light under that bushel.

In summary:

1. Van Til sees common grace as earlier grace.

2. The protecting hand of God will be removed in history.

3. This will lead to judgment of the church by evil-doers, rather than the judgment of evil-doers by God.

4. Civic righteousness will steadily disappear.

5. History is therefore a threat to Christians, Van Til says.

6. R. J. Rushdoony has adopted Van Til's view of common grace, but without showing how it can be reconciled with postmillennialism.

7. Meredith Kline has rejected Van Til's view of common grace in his attempt to reject Rushdoony's postmillennialism.

8. God grants unregenerate men favors, but not favor.

9. Christian influence will increase, while rebellious men will see their influence decrease.

10. The means of this increase in Christian influence is the extension of the rule of biblical law.

11. The universe is governed by God's law.

12. Dominion is through adherence to biblical law.

13. If unregenerate men want long-term dominion, they must obey biblical law.

14. They seek power apart from biblical law.

15. Power-seeking eventually produces impotence and historic defeat.

16. The curse of nature can be reduced through men's adherence to biblical law.

17. Without special grace, common grace cannot be maintained indefinitely.

18. As epistemological self-consciousness increases, ethical separation will increase.

19. This process brings Christians into authority.

20. There is therefore real progress in history, in every area of life.

21. The fundamental issues of life are ethical, not intellectual.

5

ESCHATOLOGY AND BIBLICAL LAW

> *But thou shalt remember the LORD thy God: for it is he that giveth thee power to get wealth, that he may establish his covenant which he sware unto thy fathers, as it is this day (Deut. 8:18).*

This verse is crucial to understanding the relationship between biblical law and compound growth over time. God grants gifts to covenantally faithful societies. These gifts are given by God in order to reinforce men's confidence in the reliability of the covenant, and so lead them to even greater faithfulness, which in turn leads to additional blessings. Visible blessings are to serve as *confirmations of the covenant.* God therefore gives men health and wealth "that he may establish his covenant." When men respond in faith and obedience, a system of *visible positive feedback* is created.

Biblical history is linear. It has a beginning (creation), meaning (sin and redemption), and an end (final judgment). It was Augustine's emphasis on linear history over pagan cyclical history that transformed the historical thinking of the West.[1]

But the biblical view of history is more than linear. It is *progressive*. It involves visible cultural expansion. It is this faith in cultural progress which has been unique to modern Western civilization. This was not due to Augustine as such, for there was an element of otherworldliness—a dualism between the progress of the soul and the rise and fall of earthly civilizations—in Augustine's view of time.[2]

It was the Reformation, and especially the Puritan vision, which brought the idea of progress to the West. The Puritans believed that there is a relationship between covenantal obedience and cultural advance.[3] This optimistic outlook was secularized by seventeenth-century Enlightenment thinkers,[4] and its waning in the twentieth century threatens the survival of Western humanistic civilization.[5]

---

1. Charles Norris Cochrane, *Christianity and Classical Culture: A Study in Thought and Action from Augustus to Augustine* (New York: Oxford University Press, [1944] 1957), pp. 480-83.

2. Herbert J. Muller, *The Uses of the Past: Profiles of Former Societies* (New York: Oxford University Press, 1957), pp. 174-75. Muller blames Augustine's dualism of body and soul on Paul, and argues that it was overcome in later Christian thinking by the recovery of the Greek heritage. This has the case precisely backwards, as Cochrane's study indicates. It was Greek thinking that was dualistic.

3. *Journal of Christian Reconstruction*, VI (Summer 1979): Symposium on Puritanism and Progress.

4. Robert A. Nisbet, "The Year 2000 and All That," *Commentary* (June 1968).

5. Robert Nisbet, *History of the Idea of Progress* (New York: Basic Books, 1980), ch. 9 and Epilogue.

Postmillennialism and Common Grace

The postmillennial system requires a doctrine of common grace and common curse. It does not require a doctrine of universal regeneration during the period of millennial blessings. In fact, no postmillennial Calvinist can afford to be without a doctrine of common grace, one which links *external* blessings to the fulfillment of *external* covenants. There has to be a period of external blessings during the final generation. Something must hold that culture together so that Satan can once again go forth and deceive the nations. The Calvinist denies that men can "lose their salvation," meaning their regenerate status. The rebels of that last day are therefore not "formerly regenerate" men. Nevertheless, they are men with power, or at least the trappings of power. They are powerful enough to delude themselves that they can destroy the people of God. And power, as I emphasize throughout this book, is not the product of antinomian or chaos-oriented philosophy. The very existence of a military chain of command demands a concept of law and order. Satan commands an army on that final day.

The postmillennial vision of the future paints a picture of historically incomparable blessings. It also tells of a final rebellion that leads to God's total and final judgment. Like the long-lived men in the days of Methuselah, judgment comes upon them in the midst of power, prosperity, and external blessings. God has been gracious to them all to the utmost of His common grace. He has been gracious in response to their covenantal faithfulness to His *civil* law-order, and He has been gracious in order to pile the maximum possible quantity of hot coals on their God-hating heads. In contrast to Van Til's amillennialist vision of the future, we must say: *when common grace is extended (not reduced) to its maximum limits possible in history, then the crack of doom has come—doom for the rebels.*

Van Til's Dilemma

Van Til destroyed any remaining hope in natural law or a common-ground philosophy. He took the insights of Abraham Kuyper and Herman Bavinck and extended these insights to their biblical and logical conclusion: *the impossibility of any natural law common ground link between covenant-keepers and covenant-breakers.* But Van Til never adopted biblical law as an alternative to the natural law systems that he so thoroughly destroyed. This always hampered the development of his own philosophy, for the older Reformed view of the moral law was based squarely on the natural-law concepts Van Til had destroyed. He was unwilling to challenge the older Reformed creeds on this point. His ideas have made creedal revisions mandatory, but he was unwilling to call publicly for a revision of the creeds leading to more biblically precise definitions of such seventeenth-century concepts as "general equity"[6] "moral law,"[7] and "the covenant of works."[8]

---

6. Westminster Confession of Faith, XIX:4.
7. Westminster Confession of Faith, XIX:5.
8. Westminster Confession of Faith, XIX:6.

There is an approach that can solve this dilemma. That is what this book attempts to do. By beginning with the concept of the covenant, we can produce a theology of common grace that recognizes the escalating ethical conflict between covenant-breakers and covenant-keepers, but which also allows for cooperation of the two through history. We must begin our inquiry with the work of the law in the sinner's heart. This must be discussed in relation to the law written in principle on regenerate hearts. A synthesis of covenant theology, eschatology, and Van Til's presuppositional apologetics makes possible a proper understanding of increasing ethical differentiation in history, but without the destruction of the foundation of history.

Victory in History

Specifically, we face the problem of victory in history. Victory in history is an inescapable concept. There can be no question of victory, either of covenant-keepers or covenant-breakers. The only question is: Who will win? If covenant-breakers rebel against biblical law, and they become externally consistent with their own antinomian presuppositions, then they will either become historically impotent (as I argue) or historically triumphant (as Van Til argues). But surely the process of differentiation leads to the victory of one or the other. There is no neutrality anywhere in the universe. This, above all, is the message of Van Til's philosophy. But if there is no intellectual and moral neutrality, then there can be no cultural, civic, or any other kind of public institutional neutrality.

Van Til argues that it is the reprobate who will
be nearly victorious in history, not the church. Only
at the end of time do the covenant-breakers face the
fact of defeat. Van Til writes: "But when all the reprobate are epistemologically self-conscious, the crack
of doom has come. The fully self-conscious reprobate will do all he can in every dimension to destroy
the people of God."[9] Yet Van Til has written in
another place that the rebel against God is like a little child who has to sit on his father's lap in order to
slap his face. How can unbelievers try to slap God's
face by slapping God's people if they are not meta-
phorically sitting on His lap? How can they get sufficient power to injure God's church if they have denied everything God teaches about how to gain and
retain power—conforming to His external laws?

What, then, can Van Til have meant by his concept of increasing epistemological self-consciousness?
Does this mean that sinners grow more consistent
with their God-denying, law-denying chaos philosophy? This seems to be what Van Til has in mind—
rebellion leading to a reduction of common grace.
But then how do these rebels gain power to do their
evil work?

As the wheat and tares grow to maturity, the
amillennialist argues, the tares become stronger and
stronger culturally, while the wheat becomes weaker
and weaker. Consider what is being said. As Christians work out their own salvation with fear and
trembling, improving their creeds, improving their

---

9. *Common Grace*, in *Common Grace and the Gospel*, p. 85.

cooperation with each other on the basis of agreement about the creeds, as they learn about the law of God as it applies in their own era, as they become skilled in applying the law of God that they have learned about, they become culturally impotent. They become infertile, also, it would seem. They do not become fruitful and multiply. Or if they do their best to follow this commandment, they are left without the blessing of God—a blessing which He has promised to those who follow the laws He has established. In short, the increase of epistemological self-consciousness on the part of Christians leads to cultural impotence.

On the other hand, as rebels develop their philosophy of antinomianism—the religion of evolutionary chaos or the religion of revolution—they become more powerful. As they depart from the presuppositions concerning God, man, law, and time that made possible Western technology and economic growth, they become richer. As they learn who they are and who God is, they appropriate the fruits of the righteous. In short, except at the day of judgment, the following Bible verse is *not* true: "A good man leaveth an inheritance to his children's children: and the wealth of the wicked is laid up for the just" (Prov. 13:22).

But what good will it do Christians after the resurrection to inherit the filthy cultural rags of the pre-resurrection world? What good will it do to have God hand back to immortal, sin-free people the accumulated wealth of anti-God, self-consistent humanists? And why would these humanists have been able to operate God's pre-resurrection world in the first place? It operates in terms of law, meaning God's covenantal law, but epistemologically self-conscious sinners would obviously refuse to abide by such covenantal laws, *assuming* that they were acting consistently with their religious presuppositions. If all of this makes no sense, it is because Van Til's concept of common grace in history makes no sense.

We need to discuss the foundation of victory in history as the Bible presents it. I tie my discussion of the principles of victory to the covenant structure of Deuteronomy. The tool of dominion that God gives to His people is His revealed law. Abandon biblical law, and you thereby abandon any hope of long-term victory. Abandon your commitment to biblical law, and you become an antinomian.

Antinomianism

The word "antinomian" is always used in a pejorative sense. It should therefore be used precisely. It is too easy to call anyone who takes a stricter view of law than you do a "legalist," and anyone who takes a more lax view an "antinomian."

We must also specify what *nomos* (law) we are talking about. Most Christians reject the label of "antinomian," and appeal to their commitment to a concept of moral law. They categorically reject the validity in New Testament times of "Hebrew judicial law," but they do this supposedly in the interests of defending a higher view of law, which they call moral law. They have been taking this approach to Old Testament civil law since the days of the early

church, and they have invariably mixed in large portions of Greek philosophy and Roman law. Such
concepts as moral law, natural law, and "cosmonomic law" have served theologians as substitutes for
biblical civil law.

What the Bible presents is a concept of God-
revealed law which possesses at least four features:
(1) permanent judicial principles, (2) concrete case-
law ordinances, (3) specification as to when and how
to apply the specific ordinance, and (4) principles of
interpretation (a hermeneutic) that inform us how
changing historical circumstances after the resurrection
have altered the specific application of ordinances. It is
not morally legitimate for Christians to seek refuge
from their God-given responsibilities to make moral
and judicial decisions. Yet they attempt to do just
this by appealing to a vague, undefined, zero-content
system of moral law that is no longer related to the
specific case-law applications of the Old Testament.

Any attempt to escape these responsibilities is a
symptom of antinomianism, that is, *anti-biblical law.*
Those who cling to a zero-content, "make up your
judicial decisions as you go along, but always in the
name of New Testament ethics" sort of moral law
have adopted a form of antinomianism.

Because theonomists reject this humanism-
influenced concept of natural law — principles of law
that are unconnected to Old Testament case laws —
Reformed theologians who have not yet understood
Van Til's rejection of all common-ground philosophy
and natural law theology have been quick to point to
the theonomists' abandonment of some of Calvin's

discussions of natural law. These critics are correct; theonomists have indeed abandoned Calvin's sixteenth-century understanding of natural law. Van Til has left them with no choice. He destroyed the intellectual case for natural law.

Natural law philosophy was pre-Darwinian humanism's crucial alternative to both biblical law and moral chaos. But there is theological progress in life, both for the saved and the lost. The more consistent humanists and the Vantillians have recognized that Darwin destroyed natural law theology and philosophy.[10] The Vantillians have also recognized that Van Til has destroyed Princeton Seminary's "common-sense realism," a disastrous eighteenth-and nineteenth-century attempt to baptize Scottish Enlightenment philosophy and rear the illegitimate infant in a Christian home.[11] Something must be built on the ruins. Theonomists have an answer: a type of covenant theology that acknowledges biblical law as the source of Christian ethics and therefore of Christian dominion.

Amillennialism's Grim Choices

I am faced with an unpleasant conclusion: *the amillennialist version of the common grace doctrine adopts either antinomianism, or a doctrine of an historically impotent gospel, or both.* It argues that God no longer

---

10. Gary North, *The Dominion Covenant: Genesis* (Tyler, Texas: Institute for Christian Economics, 1982), Appendix A: "From Cosmic Purposelessness to Humanistic Sovereignty."

11. Mark A. Noll (ed.), *The Princeton Theology, 1812-1921* (Grand Rapids, Michigan: Baker Book House, 1983).

respects His covenantal law-order, and that Deuteronomy's teaching about the positive feedback process of covenantal law is invalid in New Testament
times. The only way for the amillennialist *to avoid the
charge of antinomianism and still remain an amillennialist* is
for him to (1) abandon the concept of increasing
epistemological self-consciousness, or else (2) adopt
the doctrine of an historically impotent gospel.

Here is my reasoning. The amillennialist who insists that he is not an antinomian must proclaim the
legitimacy *and power* of biblical law. It is not enough
to claim that biblical law is ethically correct. He
must argue that God empowers the Christian to
obey it, and that this obedience produces positive
feedback. This is what the theonomic postmillennialist argues. But the amillennialist is not postmillennial, so he faces two very difficult questions: "If the
law is both legitimate and efficacious in history, then
why do Christians lose to the covenant-breakers? If
this defeat is not due to the failure of God's law, then
what does fail?" There are two escape routes.

First, if Christians fail to extend the visible manifestation of God's kingdom on earth because they do
not in fact become increasingly epistemologically
self-conscious over time, then their failure is not necessarily the failure of God's law. They ignore God's
law because they do not become epistemologically
self-conscious. They refuse to pick up God's tool of
dominion. This is not the fault of the law. So their
failure must be blamed on their lack of epistemological self-consciousness.

Second, if Christians do become increasingly

self-conscious epistemologically, as Van Til says that they will, then their failure to extend the visible kingdom must be related to (1) the fundamental weakness (or outright inapplicability) of biblical law — the assertion of antinomianism — or (2) the failure of the gospel to win men to Christ or (3) both. Either the law has failed or the gospel has failed, or both.

Deliberately Misleading Language

In any case, the amillennialist proclaims that Satan will win in history until that final day that ends history. The church fails in its mission to evangelize the world, disciple the nations, and subdue the earth to the glory of God. This is the heart and soul of the amillennialist's theory of history. *The church fails*. He may talk victory — indeed, the language of amillennialists is filled with victorious-sounding phrases — but he really means historical defeat. It is this schizophrenia of language that is so reminiscent of Barth's use of biblical terminology to promote humanism. The words do not mean what they seem. The amillennialist can no more bring himself to proclaim "the church of Jesus Christ loses in history" than the Barthian can bring himself to proclaim "the Bible is completely wrong and deliberately misleading when it speaks of a literal place called hell." They will not say clearly what they really believe.

Those of us who really do believe in the external victory of God's people in history find annoying some amillennialists' endless announcement of victory. Van Til at least avoids such language. R. B.

Kuiper's *The Glorious Body of Christ* doesn't. Chapter 42, "Conqueror of the World," is filled with the language of victory. "Amazing as it may seem, the insignificant church is out to conquer the world. Not only is it striving to do this; it is succeeding. And surpassing strange to say, not only is victory in sight for the church; it is a present reality."[12] The word "succeeding" indicates progress; the words "present reality" give away the game: in the future, we can call the church's continuing decline in influence from its present pathetic condition of cultural impotence a victory.

He includes a subsection, "The Duty of Conquest." He calls Christians to an earthly battle that his eschatology denies they can win, but he refuses to state this explicitly. He fools them with misleading language. He also includes another subsection, "The Reality of Victory." He writes: "That the church will in the end overcome the world is a foregone conclusion, for it will share in the ultimate and complete triumph of Christ, its Head."[13] This is a devious way of admitting that the church in history will *not* overcome the world in history, and that any victory it will enjoy will be post-history, when the fire of God interrupts history at the final judgment.

The church in the amillennial framework has about as much to do with this final victory of Christ over the world as a little old lady has in locking up a gang of muggers while she is being beaten to a pulp,

12. R. B. Kuiper, *The Glorious Body of Christ* (Grand Rapids, Michigan, 1958), p. 274.
13. *Ibid.*, p. 277.

when the police finally arrive. The church's role in Christ's victory is that of a helpless, impotent victim, whose only hope is that a Deliverer might arrive in the nick of time, meaning at the *end* of time. Her only hope is to be delivered from the burdens of history.

His next sentence is even more telling: "But Scripture also teaches that the church's victory over the world is a present reality." You call today's mess "victory"?

In short, he refuses to offer a biblical theory of history: an explanation of how the church gets from the visible impotence of the present to the glorious victory of the future. The church's "victory" is non-historical in the present, and it will be post-historical in the future.

Kuiper warned against the theology of Karl Barth,[14] but his view of church history—especially its future history—was essentially Barthian. Barth proclaimed two forms of history, a history of real-world events, which he called *Historie*, and Christ's world of "hidden history" (*Geschichte*, pronounced "guhSHIKtuh") —a trans-historical, non-rational encounter—that cannot be revealed by, *or judged by,* the factual records and documents of history.[15] This way, the non-"Christian" reality of history does not call into question the meaning of man's "encounter" with "Christ." Kuiper does approximately the same thing. He differ-

---

14. R. B. Kuiper, *To Be or Not to Be Reformed: Whither the Christian Reformed Church?* (Grand Rapids, Michigan: Zondervan, 1959), pp. 39, 157.

15. Van Til, *Christianity and Barthianism* (Philadelphia: Presbyterian & Reformed, 1962), ch. 1.

entiates between (1) the real historical world, where, as time goes by, you will get your Christian head kicked in by the reprobates, and (2) the above-historical world of "realized victory," which cannot be revealed by, *or judged by*, the factual historical reality of the church's increasingly visible defeat. Kuiper hides the spiritual victory of the church safely outside of the grim reality of reprobate-dominated history, just as Barth hides man's non-rational encounter with "Christ" outside of fact-based history. He proclaims a world of *Victoriegeschichte* in place of Barth's *Geschichte*. (Quite frankly, postmillennialists are sorely tempted to classify both of these dualistic theories of history as *Horsegeschichte*.)[16]

Understandably, this kind of misuse of the language of victory is annoying to those who are really serious about developing a theory of Christian victory in history. Better Van Til's forthrightness: a theory of history that openly admits that Christians, like that little old lady, are going to get mugged, and mugged ever-more frequently and ever-more viciously.

Reprobation by Knowledge?

Van Til writes: "But when all the reprobate are epistemologically self-conscious, the crack of doom has come. The fully self-conscious reprobate will do all he can in every dimension to destroy the people of God. So while we seek with all our power to hasten the process of differentiation in every dimension, we are yet thankful, on the other hand, for 'the day of

---

16. You know: horsing around with historical facts.

grace,' the day of undeveloped differentiation. Such tolerance as we receive on the part of the world is due to this fact that we live in the earlier, rather than the later, stage of history."[17]

Consider the implications of this argument. Presenting the gospel to unregenerate men helps to make them more aware of what they are and who they are. But at this earlier stage of history, this degree of self-awareness on their part is not so great that they seek to suppress Christians, just as they do not yet fully attempt to suppress the testimony of God to them in the revelation of the creation and also the Bible.

Later, however, as this self-awareness of the unregenerate increases, and they adhere more and more to their religious and philosophical premises concerning the origins of matter out of chaos, and the ultimate return of all matter into pure randomness, this vision of ultimate chaos somehow makes them more confident, unlike the visible breakdown in self-confidence that just this sort of philosophy is producing today in the West. They will begin to persecute the church. Things will go from bad to worse for the church as the church attempts to present more people with the gospel. The more the unregenerate hear, the more they will be able to suppress the church. Van Til therefore says that there is a good reason to rejoice that we live today rather than tomorrow. Van Til really does understand the implications of amillennialism.

---

17. *Common Grace*, in *Common Grace and the Gospel*, p. 85.

On the other hand, the Christians are humble before God, but confident before the creation which they are called by God to subdue. After all, they have biblical law and the Holy Spirit. This confidence eventually leads the Christians into historic defeat and disaster, say those amillennialists who believe in increasing epistemological self-consciousness.

In contrast to the ever-weakening band of faithful covenant-keepers, the ethical rebels are arrogant before God, and claim that all nature is ruled by the meaningless laws of probability—ultimate chaos, including moral chaos. By immersing themselves in the philosophy of chaos, covenant-breakers will somehow be able to emerge totally victorious across the whole face of the earth, says the amillennialist, a victory which is called to a halt only by the physical intervention of Jesus Christ at the final judgment. A commitment to lawlessness, in the amillennial version of common grace, leads to external victory. This makes no sense theologically, let alone morally, yet it is consistent with Van Til's explanation of declining common grace over time. Where did he go wrong?

Van Til is correct when he writes that there will be an increase in everyone's self-knowledge, or what he calls *epistemological self-consciousness*. Saved and lost will become increasingly aware of just where they stand philosophically and ethically, and who they are historically. But Van Til has erred in an important point. As a Christian philosopher, he knows that salvation is not by knowledge. The Greeks were incorrect when they argued that if a man knows the good, he will do the good. Paul says precisely the opposite:

a person can know the good, but still do evil (Rom. 7).

What Van Til never openly admits is this: neither is *reprobation* by knowledge, including self-knowledge. It is not simply that evil men know the good but refuse to do it; it is that they know the bad, but it is not bad enough for them.

Evil's Lever: Good

Covenant-breakers must do good externally in order to increase their ability to do evil. They need to use the lever of God's law in order to increase their influence. These rebels will not be able to act consistently with their own epistemological presuppositions and still be able to exercise power. They want power more than they want philosophical consistency. This is especially true of Western covenant-breakers who live in the shadow of Christian dominion theology. In short, *they restrain the working out of the implications of their own epistemological self-consciousness.* Believers in randomness, chaos, and meaningless, the power-seekers nevertheless choose structure, discipline, and the rhetoric of ultimate victory.

If a modern investigator would like to see as fully consistent a pagan culture as one might imagine, he could visit the African tribe, the Ik ("eek"). Colin Turnbull did, and his book, *The Mountain People* (1973), is a classic. He found almost total rebellion against law—family law, civic law, all law. Yet he also found a totally impotent, beaten tribal people who were rapidly becoming extinct. They were harmless to the West because they were more self-consistent that the West's satanists.

The difference between the humanist power-seekers and the more fully consistent but suicidal tribal pagans is the difference between the Communists and the Ik. It is the difference between power religion and escape religion.[18] Some Eastern mystic who seeks escape through ascetic techniques of withdrawal, or some Western imitator with an alpha wave machine and earphones ("Become an instant electronic yogi!"), is acting far more consistently with the anti-Christian philosophy of ultimate meaninglessness than a Communist revolutionary is. The yogi is not fully consistent: he still needs discipline techniques, and discipline implies an orderly universe. But he is more consistent than the Communist. He is not seeking the salvation of a world of complete illusion (maya) through the exercise of power.

Satan needs a chain of command in order to exercise power. Thus, in order to create the greatest havoc for the church, Satan and his followers need to imitate the church. Like the child who needs to sit on his father's lap in order to slap him, so does the rebel need a crude imitation of God's dominion theology in order to exercise power. A child who rejects the idea of his father's lap cannot seriously hope to slap him. The anti-Christian has officially adopted an "anti-lap" theory of existence. He admits no cause-and-effect relationship between lap and slap. To the extent that he acts consistently with this view, he becomes impotent to attack God's people.

---

18. Gary North, *Moses and Pharaoh: Dominion Religion vs. Power Religion* (Tyler, Texas: Institute for Christian Economics, 1985), Introduction.

This means that with an increase in epistemological self-consciousness, the *ethical* aspects of the separation become more and more fundamental. Not logic but ethics is primary. Reprobation is by ethics, not logic. Thus, the increasing epistemological self-consciousness on the part of the power-seeking unbeliever does not lead him to *apply* Satan's philosophy of ultimate meaninglessness and chaos; it leads him instead to apply Satan's counterfeit of dominion religion, the religion of power. He can achieve power only by refusing to become fully consistent with Satan's religion of chaos. He needs organization and capital—God's gifts of common grace—in order to produce maximum destruction. Like the Soviet Union, which has always had to import or steal the bulk of its technology from the West in order to build up an arsenal to destroy the West,[19] so does the satanist have to import Christian intellectual and moral capital in order to wage an effective campaign against the church.

This is the key point in my argument against Van Til's view of common grace. First, the Christian exercises dominion by becoming epistemologically self-conscious, meaning morally and logically con-

---

19. Antony Sutton, *The Best Enemy Money Can Buy* (Billings, Montana: Liberty House, 1986). On the technological dependence of the Soviet Union on commercial Western imports, see also Sutton, *Western Technology and Soviet Economic Development*, 3 Volumes (Stanford, California: Hoover Institution Press, 1968-73); Charles Levinson, *Vodka Cola* (New York: Gordon & Cremonesi, 1978); Joseph Finder, *Red Carpet* (New York: Holt, Rinehart & Winston, 1983).

sistent with the new man within him, and therefore by adhering ever more closely to God's law. Biblical law is the covenant-keeper's *fully self-consistent tool of dominion.*

Second, the covenant-breaker exercises power by becoming *inconsistent* with his ultimate philosophy of randomness. He can commit effective crimes only by *stealing the worldview of Christians.* The bigger the crimes he wishes to commit (the ethical impulse of evil), the more carefully he must plan (the epistemological impulse of righteousness: counting the costs [Luke 14:28-30]). The Christian can work to fulfill the dominion covenant through a life of consistent thought and action; the anti-Christian can achieve an offensive, destructive campaign against the Christians—as contrasted to a self-destructive life of drugs and debauchery—only by stealing the biblical worldview and twisting it to evil purposes.

In short, *to become really evil you need to become pretty good.*

The Bible says that all those who hate God love death (Prov. 8:36b). Therefore, for God-haters to live consistently, they would have to commit suicide. It is not surprising that the French existentialist philosopher Albert Camus was fascinated with the possibility of suicide. It was consistent with his philosophy of meaninglessness. To become a historic threat to Christians, unbelievers must *restrain their own ultimate impulse,* namely, the quest for death. Thus, their increase in epistemological self-consciousness over time is incomplete, until the final rebellion, when their very act of rebellion brings on the final judgment. It will be the final culmination in history of Satan's earlier act of envious defiance in luring the mobs to crucify Christ: an act of violence that insured his total judgment and defeat. Yet he did it anyway, out of spite. When God finally removes His restraint on their suicidal impulse, they will launch their suicidal rebellion. The removal of God's restraint is always a prelude to judgment.

Van Til views Satan's actions at the cross as an intellectual failure. "Satan managed to have Christ crucified in order to destroy him. Did he not know that by the crucifixion of Christ his own kingdom would be destroyed? So we see that though, on the one hand, Satan's power of ingenuity is great, he constantly frustrates himself in his purposes; he is constantly mistaken in his knowledge of reality."[20] But was it Satan's erroneous knowledge of reality that thwarted him? "Did he not know?" Van Til asks rhetorically. Of course he knew. He did not make a mistake. He simply saw an opportunity to get even temporarily, and he took it, no matter what the cost. Reprobation is not by knowledge. Reprobation is by ethics. *Satan is suicidal*, not irrational. He is envy-driven, not stupid.

So the ethical war will escalate. Whom should we expect God to bless in this escalating ethical war? The Christian whose worldview is consistent and God-honoring, or the God-hater whose worldview is inconsistent and God-defying? Who will be burdened by greater moral and intellectual schizophrenia as

---

20. *An Introduction to Systematic Theology*, pp. 91-92.

time goes on and epistemological self-consciousness increases? Whose plans of conquest will be inconsistent with his philosophy of existence, the Christian or the anti-Christian? Who is truly growing in epistemological self-consciousness, the Christian or the anti-Christian?

The answers should be obvious. Unfortunately for Reformed theological scholarship in the twentieth century, amillennialism makes the obvious obscure, and amillennialism has been the dominant Reformed eschatology since the 1930's.

Amillennialism Has Things Backwards

It should be clear by now that the amillennialist version of the relationship between biblical law and the creation is completely backwards. No doubt Satan wishes it were a true version. No doubt he wants his followers to believe that by progressively adhering to biblical law, Christians will fall into increasing cultural impotence. No doubt he wants his followers to believe this preposterous error. But how can a consistent Christian believe it? How can a Christian believe that adherence to biblical law produces cultural impotence, while commitment to philosophical chaos—the religion of satanic revolution—leads to cultural victory?

There is no doubt in my mind that the amillennialists do not want to teach such a doctrine, yet that is where their amillennial pessimism inevitably leads. Dutch Calvinists preach the continuing New Testament validity of the cultural mandate (dominion covenant),[21] yet they simultaneously preach that this mandate from God cannot be fulfilled in history. They refuse to acknowledge the future reality of Christian dominion on earth before the final judgment by means of the *positive feedback* aspect of covenantal blessings: from obedience to blessing to greater obedience.

Biblical law is basic to the fulfillment of the cultural mandate. It is our tool of dominion. There are only four possibilities concerning law: revealed law, natural law, chaos, or a syncretistic combination of the above (e.g., statistical regularity: a little natural law and a little randomness). The amillennial tradition has outspokenly denied the first possibility: the binding character of Old Testament law in New Testament times. We do not find treatises on the contemporary application of biblical law written by amillennialist theologians. Therefore, the amillennialist who preaches the obligation of trying to fulfill the cultural mandate (which he also says cannot be fulfilled in history) apart from the tool of biblical law thereby plunges himself either into the camp of the chaos cults (mystics, revolutionaries), or into the camp of the natural-law, common-ground philosophers, or into a truly schizophrenic camp which teaches a mixture of verbal mysticism and natural law. (I have in mind the Dooyeweerdian "cosmonomic law" philosophy.)

---

21. Abraham Kuyper, *Lectures on Calvinism* (Grand Rapids, Michigan: Eerdmans, [1898] 1931); Henry R. Van Til, *The Calvinistic Concept of Culture* (Philadelphia: Presbyterian & Reformed, 1959).

Dooyeweerd's Mysticism

This leads me to my next point. It is somewhat
speculative and may not be completely accurate. It is
an idea which ought to be pursued, however, to see if
it is accurate. I think that the reason why the philosophy of Herman Dooyeweerd, the Dutch philosopher of law, had some temporary impact in Dutch
Calvinist intellectual circles in the late 1960's and
early 1970's is that Dooyeweerd's theory of sphere
sovereignty — sphere laws that are *not* to be filled in
by means of revealed, Old Testament law[22] — is consistent with the amillennial (Dutch) version of the
cultural mandate. Dooyeweerd's system and Dutch
amillennialism are essentially antinomian: against
biblical law. This is why I wrote my 1967 essay,
"Social Antinomianism," in response to the Dooyeweerdian professor at the Free University of Amster-
dam, A. Troost.[23]

Either the Dooyeweerdians wind up as mystics,
or else they try to create a new kind of "common-
ground philosophy" to link believers and unbeliev-

---

22. Dooyeweerd rejects Van Til's call to think God's thoughts
after Him, to structure the categories of philosophy in terms of
the Bible. Dooyeweerd goes so far as to assert: "Nowhere does
the Bible speak of obeying the voice of God in terms of subjecting
every human thought to divine thought." Dooyeweerd, in E. R.
Geehan (ed.), *Jerusalem & Athens: Critical Discussions on the Theology and Apologetics of Cornelius Van Til* (Nutley, New Jersey: Presbyterian & Reformed, 1971), p. 84. He then lapses into his familiar garbled mysticism concerning the "heart" as "the religious
center of our existence."

23. Gary North, *The Sinai Strategy: Economics and the Ten Commandments* (Tyler, Texas: Institute for Christian Economics,
1986), Appendix C: "Social Antinomianism."

ers. Sometimes they try to do both. Their language is the language of mysticism, but their strategy is common-ground. It was Dooyeweerd's outspoken resistance to Old Testament and New Testament authority over the *content* of his hypothesized sphere laws that has led his increasingly radical, increasingly antinomian followers into anti-Christian paths.

Van Til recognized this lack of content in Dooyeweerd's methodology,[24] just as he recognized the common-ground nature of Dooyeweerd's system,[25] but since he himself never developed an apologetic method based on the covenantal requirements of revealed biblical law, he could not thrust an exegetical stake into Dooyeweerd's epistemological "heart." Like Dracula rising from the dead, Dooyeweerd's philosophy keeps making reappearances, though increasingly dressed up in the guerilla uniforms worn by safely tenured professors of liberation theology— "designer camouflage," one might say.

Amillennialists have preached the dominion covenant ("cultural mandate"), and then have turned around and denied the efficacy of biblical law in culture. They necessarily deny the cultural efficacy of biblical law because their eschatological interpretation has led them to conclude that there can be no external, cultural victory in time and on earth by faithful Christians. Epistemological self-consciousness will increase, but things only get worse over

---

24. Van Til, "Response," *Jerusalem and Athens*, p. 112.
25. *Ibid.*, pp. 102-3.

time. Biblical law, even when empowered by the Holy Spirit, is culturally impotent.

Kline vs. Bahnsen

If you preach that biblical law produces "positive feedback," both personally and culturally—that God rewards covenant-keepers and punishes covenant-breakers in history—then you are preaching a system of positive growth. You are preaching the progressive fulfillment dominion covenant. Only if you deny that there is any long-term sustainable relationship between external covenant-keeping and external success in life—a denial made explicit by Meredith G. Kline[26]—can you escape from the postmillennial implications of biblical law.

This is why it is odd that Greg Bahnsen insists on presenting his defense of biblical law apart from his well-known postmillennialism. "What these studies

---

26. Meredith Kline says that any connection between blessings and covenant-keeping is, humanly speaking, random. "And meanwhile it [the common grace order] must run its course within the uncertainties of the mutually conditioning principles of common grace and common curse, prosperity and adversity being experienced in a manner largely unpredictable because of the inscrutable sovereignty of the divine will that dispenses them in mysterious ways." Kline, "Comments on the Old-New Error," *Westminster Theological Journal*, XLI (Fall 1978), p. 184. Dr. Kline has obviously never considered just why it is that life insurance premiums and health insurance premiums are cheaper in Christian-influenced societies than in pagan societies. Apparently, the blessings of long life that are promised in the Bible are sufficiently non-random and "scrutable" that statisticians who advise insurance companies can detect statistically relevant differences between societies.

present is a position in Christian (normative) *ethics*. They do *not* logically commit those who agree with them to any particular school of *eschatological* interpretation."[27] He is correct: *logically*, there is no connection. *Covenantally*, the two doctrines are inescapable: when biblical law is preached, believed, and obeyed, there must be blessings; blessings lead inescapably to victory.

Perhaps he has decided that it is unwise to try to fight a two-front war: theonomy and postmillennialism. (My attitude is that it is giving away the battle not to fight on both fronts simultaneously, which is what this book is about.) On the other hand, perhaps he wanted to narrow the focus of his discussion of ethics to the question of the rightness or wrongness, biblically speaking, of adopting biblical law in New Testament times, without any consideration of the historical consequences of the covenantal process of positive feedback (Deut. 8:18). If this was his intention, then his books go too far down the road toward the issue of the empowering of Christians to obey biblical law. As soon as you raise this issue of the Spirit's empowering, you raise the unified issue of positive feedback, external growth, and long-term victory.

To escape the postmillennial implications of this argument, the defender of theonomy (God's law) would have to argue that the preaching of the law does not *necessarily* have to produce a faithful, sus-

27. Greg L. Bahnsen, *By This Standard: The Authority of God's Law Today* (Tyler, Texas: Institute for Christian Economics, 1985), p. 8.

tainable response in the hearts and lives of people over time. Positive feedback between covenantal faithfulness and covenantal blessings can still be broken, the defender would admit, just as it was broken every time in the Old Testament. Theologically, it is possible for an amillennial or a premillennial defender of biblical law to argue this way, and I know a handful in both camps who do, but Bahnsen's particular defense of theonomy makes such an argument difficult to sustain.

Empowering by the Spirit

He has argued repeatedly that what distinguishes biblical law in the New Testament era from the Old Covenant era is the vastly greater empowering of Christians by the Holy Spirit to obey the law.[28]

I agree entirely with this argument. The Spirit's empowering is a fundamental distinction between the two covenantal periods. It is also interesting to note that the only broad-based acceptance of the theonomic position is taking place in charismatic circles—circles in which the positive power of the Holy Spirit is stressed. But this greater empowering by the Spirit must be made manifest in history if it is to be distinguished from the repeated failure of believers in the Old Covenant era to stay in the "positive feedback" mode: blessings . . . greater faith . . . greater blessings, etc. It is this positive feedback aspect of biblical law in New Testament times which links

28. *Ibid.*, pp. 159-62, 185-86. Cf. Bahnsen, *Theonomy in Christian Ethics* (2nd ed.; Phillipsburg, New Jersey: Presbyterian & Reformed, 1984), ch. 4.

"theonomy" with postmillennialism (though not necessarily postmillennialism with theonomy: see chapter six on the antinomian theology of Jonathan Edwards).

Bahnsen has argued forcefully that any discussion of the expansion of God's kingdom must include a discussion of the visible manifestations of this kingdom. To speak of the kingdom of God without being able to point to its expansion of influence outside the narrow confines of the institutional church is misleading.[29] This argument also is correct.

But what of a parallel argument? If we were to argue that the greater empowering of the Holy Spirit in the New Testament era is only a kind of theoretical backdrop to history, and therefore biblical law will not actually be preached and obeyed in this pre-final-judgment age (which is the amillennialist argument), then we would really be abandoning the whole idea of the Holy Spirit's empowering of Christians and Christian society in history. It would be an argument analogous to the kingdom arguments of the amillennialist: "Yes, God has a kingdom, and Christians are part of it, and it is a victorious kingdom; however, there are no visible signs of the King or His kingdom, and Christians will be increasingly defeated in history." Similarly, "Yes, the Spirit empowers Christians to obey biblical law; however, they will not adopt or obey biblical law in history."

29. Greg Bahnsen, "This World and the Kingdom of God," *Christian Reconstruction*, VIII (Sept./Oct., 1986), published by the Institute for Christian Economics.

Will the progressive manifestation of the fruits of obeying biblical law also be strictly internal? If so, then what has happened to the positive feedback aspect of covenant law? What has happened to empowering by the Holy Spirit?

I would argue that the greater empowering by the Holy Spirit for God's people to obey and enforce biblical law is what invalidates the implicit amillennialist position regarding the ineffectiveness of biblical law in New Testament times. If Christians obey it, then the positive feedback process is inevitable; it is part of the theonomic aspect of the creation: "from victory unto victory." If some segments of the church refuse to obey it, then those segments will eventually lose influence, money, and power. Their place will be taken by those Christian churches that obey God's laws, and that will therefore experience the covenant's external blessings. These churches will spread the gospel more effectively as a result. This is the positive feedback aspect of biblical law.

Kline attacked both of Bahnsen's doctrines — biblical law and postmillennialism — in his critique of *Theonomy*,[30] but Bahnsen judiciously responded to Kline's criticisms of his postmillennial eschatology only in an "addendum," stating explicitly that he did not regard this aspect of Kline's critique as logically relevant to the topic of theonomy.[31] But Kline was

---

30. Kline, *op. cit.*
31. Greg L. Bahnsen, "M. G. Kline on Theonomic Politics: An Evaluation of His Reply," *Journal of Christian Reconstruction*, VI (Winter 1979-80), "Addendum: Kline's Critique of Postmillennialism." Bahnsen writes: "Although Kline's polemic against

covenantally correct: there is unquestionably a necessary connection in New Testament times between
a covenantal concept of biblical law and postmillennial eschatology. Kline rejects the idea of a New Testament covenantal law-order, and he also rejects
postmillennialism. Kline and his fellow amillennialists are consistent in their rejection of both biblical
law and postmillennialism. Postmillennialists should
be equally consistent in linking the two positions.
We must argue covenantally, and this necessarily involves the question of the positive feedback of covenantal blessings and the church's empowering by the
Holy Spirit.

If we accept the possibility of a defense of God's
law that rejects the historic inevitability of the long-
term expansion of Christian dominion through the
covenant's positive feedback, then we face a major
problem, the one Bahnsen's theory of the empowering by the Spirit has raised: *how to explain the difference
between the New Testament church and Old Testament
Israel*. If the Christian church fails to build the visible
kingdom by means of biblical law and the power of
the gospel, despite the resurrection of Christ and the
presence of the Holy Spirit, then what kind of religion are we preaching? Why is the church a significant improvement culturally and socially over Old
Testament Israel?

What does such a theology say about the gospel?

---

postmillennialism is not logically or theologically relevant to his
debate with me over socio-political ethics, some readers may be
interested in a brief response to this aspect of his article as well"
(p. 215). He then devotes six pages to the topic.

What kind of power does the gospel offer men for the overcoming of the effects of sin in history? Is Satan's one-time success in tempting Adam never going to be overcome in history? Will Satan attempt to comfort himself throughout eternity with the thought that by defeating Adam, he made it impossible for mankind to work out the dominion covenant in history, even in the face of the death and resurrection of Christ? If we argue this way—the failure of a Spirit-empowered biblical law-order to produce the visible kingdom—then we must find an answer to this question: Why is sin triumphant in history, in the face of the gospel?

Then there is the impolite but inevitable question: *Why is Jesus a loser in history?*

And, just for the record, let me ask another question: "When in history will we see the fulfillment of the promise of Isaiah 32, when churls will no longer be called liberal, generous people shall no longer be called churls, and (presumably) the historic defeat of the church will no longer be called the victory of God's kingdom?"

Preaching External Defeat

Amillennialists, by preaching eschatological impotence culturally, thereby immerse themselves in quicksand—the quicksand of antinomianism. Some sands are quicker than others. Eventually, they swallow up anyone so foolish as to try to walk through them. Antinomianism leads into the pits of impotence and retreat. No one wants to risk everything he owns, including his life, in a battle his commander says will not be won. Only a few diehard souls will attempt it. You can build a ghetto with such a theology; you cannot build a civilization.

Amillennial Calvinists will continue to be plagued by Dooyeweerdians, mystics, natural-law compromisers, and antinomians of all sorts until they finally abandon their amillennial eschatology. Furthermore, biblical law must also be preached. It must be seen as the tool of cultural reconstruction. It must be seen as operating *now*, in New Testament times. It must be seen that there is a relationship between covenantal faithfulness and obedience to law — that without obedience there is no faithfulness, no matter how emotional believers may become, or how sweet the gospel tastes (for a while). Furthermore, there are external blessings that follow covenantal obedience to God's law-order.

Premillennialism and Biblical Law

Perhaps I should devote an entire chapter on this subject, but I do not think it warrants the space. That dispensational premillennialism rejects Old Testament law for this dispensation, the Church Age, is well known. The entire hermeneutic of dispensationalism is based on radical discontinuities in God's dealing with people in seven (or thereabouts) different dispensations. Biblical law does not apply to our dispensation.

It is true, they admit, that biblical law will be reinstated in the post-Rapture millennial age, for an Old Testament-type theocracy under Jesus will be set up. Nevertheless, there will be a final rebellion of

Satan at the end of the millennium. I have never
seen any discussion by a dispensationalist concerning the relationship between common grace and this
final satanic outbreak. Will common grace at last
trigger Satan's rebellion? I have seen no premillennial author tackle this question. I suspect that such a
theory of Satan's rebellion would be consistent with
dispensationalism, but generally dispensationalist
discussions of the final rebellion have more to do
with God's simply allowing Satan more chain to
hang himself with. (I also think they have in mind a
more literal chain than covenant theologians do:
Rev. 20:1-3.)

In any case, a theology of common grace would
be difficult to apply consistently to a post-Rapture
millennial era in which resurrected, sin-free, non-
reproducing, eternal Christians are working side by side
with sinful, mortal, redeemed and unredeemed people. I suppose such a theology could be constructed
as an academic exercise, but there would be no commercial market for the published results. This sort of
hypothetical question has little to do with building a
strategy for the church prior to the Rapture.

What is significant for the discussion at hand is
that *with respect to our own era, prior to Christ's return and
the Rapture of the saints*, as we also find in all amillennial systems, the church fails in its task of worldwide
dominion. The world is not going to be filled with
Christians who exercise visible cultural dominion,
this side of the Rapture. The covenant's positive
feedback relationship between external adherence to
biblical law and external dominion supposedly does

not operate in this premillennial era. In this respect, premillennialists agree with amillennialists.

Very few premillennialists have thought about (let alone written about) the concept of common grace. It has no practical relevance to premillennial theology. Few premillennialists believe that we are still under the terms of the dominion covenant. The premillennial Bible Presbyterian Church in 1970 categorically denied the New Testament validity of the cultural mandate.[32]

If some premillennialist does have a theory of common grace which applies to the church age, meaning history this side of the Rapture, it would have to be similar to the amillennialist version. It would deny the relevance of the positive feedback process of covenantal blessings. Nevertheless, it would at least be more consistent than the amillennial version. Since the cultural mandate is no longer in force, according to most premillennialists, the schizophrenic and frustrating program of Dutch amillennialism is absent: at least premillennialists do not feel called by God to do what God says cannot and will not be done in history anyway. The premillennialist says that the cultural victory of Bible-believing people will come on earth only after the great discontinuous event of the Rapture. This is "the blessed hope." It will be exclusively God's work. The church is off the hook.

"Off the hook." This is the heart and soul of pre-

---

32. R. J. Rushdoony, *The Institutes of Biblical Law* (Nutley, New Jersey: Craig Press, 1973), pp. 723-24.

millennial social ethics. Amillennialists are on the hook.

As Rushdoony once remarked to me, amillennialists are simply premillennialists without earthly hope.

C. S. Lewis

C. S. Lewis understood that there is a war going on between Christ and Satan. His magnificent novel, *That Hideous Strength*, subtitled *A Modern Fairy-Tale for Grown-Ups*, deals with the fusion of magic, technology, and the demonic quest for power. Perhaps better than any Christian writer of this century, he understood Satan and Satan's mode of operations.

We cannot say as much for his understanding of Christianity. His theology was muddled, at best, and his epistemology was clearly a mixture of Platonism and the Bible. So we would not normally go to Lewis to discover a solution to our problems. We go to him for an understanding of our era, however.

His view of history was very much like Van Til's. He believed in the increase of epistemological self-consciousness over time. This progress over time removes the latitude for making moral decisions, for the issues of life become clearer. Here is a speech given by a college professor (possibly modeled after Lewis himself) in *That Hideous Strength*: "If you dip into any college, or school, or parish, or family—anything you like—at a given point in its history, you always find that there was a time before that point when there was more elbow room and contrasts weren't quite so sharp; and that there's going to be a time after that point when there is even less room for indecision and choices are even more momentous. Good is always getting better and bad is always getting worse: the possibilities of even apparent neutrality are always diminishing. The whole thing is sorting itself out all the time, coming to a point, getting sharper and harder."[33]

The problem with Lewis' outlook is that he never suggested any way that Christians could make these moral decisions in the public realm. He told us of the war, told us that we would not be able to escape our responsibilities, told us that our decisions would become ever-clearer, and yet refused to offer any hope that the public issues of any era could be solved by an appeal to the Bible. Indeed, he specifically rejected such a suggestion.

He dismissed as unrealizable the creation of any distinct or distinctly Christian political party—a long-time ideal of many Dutch Christians. Christians do not agree on the means of attaining the proper goals of society, he argued. A Christian political party will wind up in a deadlock, or else the winning faction will force all rivals out. Then it will no longer be representative of Christians in society. So this minority party will attach itself to the nearest non-Christian political party.

The problem as Lewis saw it is that the party will speak for Christendom, but will not in fact represent all of Christendom. "By the mere act of calling itself

---

33. C. S. Lewis, *That Hideous Strength: A Modern Fairy-Tale for Grown-Ups* (New York: Macmillan, [1946] 1979), p. 283.

the Christian Party it implicitly accuses all Christians who do not join it of apostasy and betrayal. It will be exposed, in an aggravated degree, to that temptation which the Devil spares none of us at any time—the temptation of claiming for our favourite opinions that kind of degree of certainty and authority which really belongs only to our Faith."[34]

This is an odd line of argumentation. First, what he describes as a strictly political problem is in fact the problem with any distinctly Christian institution. Christians need to do what is God's will, but in doing it, they exclude other acts as not being in God's will. Yet according to his view of history, these decisions will become clearer over time, and the range of Christian (as well as non-Christian) choices will become much narrower. So what is the problem? It should be easier as time goes on to build Christian institutions of all kinds, not just political organizations.

Second, why doesn't this same problem of speaking in the name of the accepted moral sovereign afflict every religious, political, or ideological group? Why single out politics? Isn't ascertaining God's will equally a problem in all other institutions? Furthermore, why are Christian political coalitions so evil, so doomed to defeat? Aren't coalitions going on in every area of life all the time? Besides, why is the problem of coalitions a uniquely Christian problem? Humanists make coalitions all the time—yes, even

---

34. C. S. Lewis, *God in the Dock: Essays on Theology and Ethics* (Grand Rapids, Michigan: Eerdmans, 1970), p. 198.

highly ideological humanists. Coalitions are basic to life.

What he is really saying is that humanists can run their institutions and our lives just fine, but Christians cannot — not because Christians are presently incompetent, but simply because they are Christians.

He argues that anyone who adds "Thus said the Lord" to his earthly utterances will insist that his conscience speaks more clearly "the more it is loaded with sin. And this comes from pretending that God has spoken when He has not spoken." *Hath God said?* That was what Satan asked Eve. But God *had* said. And He has spoken to us, too: in His Bible. Dare we deny His words? Eve dared. See where it got her. And us. But Lewis feared those who speak concretely to real-world problems in the name of God.

We are back to Barthianism. God's will in history cannot be conveyed in cognitive sentences, creeds, political programs, economics, or anything else in this scientific, factual universe. God does not speak to specific problems in history. This is the essence of Barthianism. It is also the essence of antinomianism.

Perhaps Lewis was willing to accept creeds as God's word, but creeds are written by Christians who disagree with other Christians. That is the function of creeds: to separate (exclude) wrong-thinking Christians from better-thinking Christians. Creeds are hammered out in the midst of controversy, sometimes including political controversy, and sometimes even life-and-death controversy. Are we to deny, as Barth did, that God speaks cognitively to men in

creeds? Deny that God speaks to any area of life, and
you have denied God's jurisdiction in that area of
life. Deny that men are responsible before God for
searching out God's will and then working to apply
it, and you have adopted the theology of mysticism.

Then how are Christians to make moral decisions? Lewis appeals to that old Stoic standby, natural
law. "By the natural light He has shown us what
means are lawful: to find out which one is efficacious
He has given us brains. The rest He left to us."[35]

In short, do your own natural thing, but do not
do it in the name of Jesus.

What he recommended was an interdenomina-
tional voters society whose members will write letters
to their political representatives. They will "pester"
the politicians. But in whose name should they pester them? In God's name? If not, then haven't Christians become just another special-interest group with
no distinctly Christian platform?

But he did offer some hope—a postmillennial
hope. He ends the essay with these words: "There is
a third way—by becoming a majority. He who converts his neighbour has performed the most practical
Christian political act of all."

What can we make of all this? He said that
choices in life will become more epistemologically
self-conscious. He was afraid of politicians who
speak in God's name. He appealed to natural reason. He told Christians to pester politicians. Then
he said to spread the gospel and become a majority.

---

35. *Ibid.*, p. 199.

What then?

It is all a muddle, but at least it is a four-page muddle. The endless publications of those who call for Christian relevance in society, but who refuse to turn to biblical law as God's inspired "platform" in every area of responsibility, are no less muddled than Lewis, and far more verbose.

The principle is simple enough: *no law of God, no jurisdiction of God*. Until Christians get this straight in their thinking, they will remain either Christian activists who are publicly muddled and culturally irrelevant, or else Christian retreatists who are privately muddled and culturally irrelevant.

Conclusion

Those who are ethically subordinate to Satan can nevertheless receive external blessings if they obey God's law externally. At the final day, they will rebel. Thus, the postmillennialist does not preach that the whole world will someday be populated exclusively by regenerate people. But because he affirms that the whole world will experience cultural blessings as a result of the spread of the gospel, the postmillennialist needs to have a doctrine of common grace, in order to explain the final rebellion without having to adopt an Arminian doctrine of a fall from grace, meaning special grace.

By denying the legitimacy of Old Testament law in New Testament times, amillennialists thereby abandon the tool of dominion which God has given to His people to fulfill the terms of the dominion covenant ("cultural mandate"). They have abandoned

God's program of "positive feedback" — the progressive sanctification of civilization. They have therefore abandoned an eschatology of victory in history.

Which is the primary impulse of amillennialism, its defeatist eschatology or its antinomianism? It is possible to make a good case for either. I think antinomianism is the primary impulse. If the conditional promises of Deuteronomy 28:1-14 are taken seriously, and our empowering by the Holy Spirit is taken seriously, then the doctrine of historical progress can be taken seriously. This progress must become externalized through the biblical system of positive feedback (Deut. 8:18). To deny such historical, institutional progress, the amillennialist must reject biblical law. Postmillennialism is "a nice dream," as one Protestant Reformed Church pastor said from the pulpit. Amillennialists can afford to ignore nice dreams. Biblical law, on the other hand, involves a direct assault on pietism, humanism, mysticism, and all other versions of the escape religion. It cannot be ignored. It calls men out of their monastic cloisters, their ghettos, and their sanctuaries. Preach biblical law, and you will not be dismissed as a dreamer; you will be challenged as a fanatic. I think antinomianism is the underlying motive of amillennialism.

A war is in progress — a war with humanism. Humanism will not respect Christian sanctuaries. Humanism must be defeated. Biblical law is the weapon, with Christians empowered by the Holy Spirit. If you have no weapons, you have an excuse not to fight. You run for your ghetto. As the Jews learned in Warsaw, this strategy has distinct limits. So the theonomists call men to pick up God's weapon, biblical law, to carry with them when they bring the gospel to the lost. There can be no more excuses for cultural impotence. Christians have the tool of dominion. It will do no good to say that Christians cannot win in history, for we have the weapons to win. Any excuse now is simply an unwillingness to join the battle. But as in the days of Deborah, there are many who choose not to fight. And some day, some future Deborah will sing a modern version of: "Gilead abode beyond Jordan: and why did Dan remain in ships? Asher continued on the sea shore, and abode in his breaches [inlets]" (Jud. 5:17).

If progress is seen as exclusively internal, or at most ecclesiastical, as it is in all forms of amillennialism, then history inescapably becomes antinomian. Biblical law must be abandoned. *Biblical law in New Testament times does not permit long-term failure.* Biblical law necessarily must lead to positive visible results, which in turn should reinforce faithfulness, as well as serve as a light to the unconverted (Deut. 4:6-8), a city on a hill (Matt. 5:14). Amillennialism implicitly denies that a biblical city on a hill will be built. There will only be congregations in the catacombs, groups in the Gulag. Van Til makes this plain. Once more, I cite his uncompromising analysis:

But when all the reprobate are epistemologically self-conscious, the crack of doom has come. The fully self-conscious reprobate will do all he can in every dimension to destroy the people of God. So while we seek with all our power to hasten the process of differentiation in every dimension we are yet thankful, on the other hand, for "the day of grace," the day of undeveloped differentiation. Such tolerance as we receive on the part of the world is due to this fact that we live in the earlier, rather than in the later, stage of history. And such influence on the public situation as we can effect, whether in society or in state, presupposes this undifferentiated stage of development.[36]

As time goes on, Christians lose. Van Til has therefore accepted the eschatology of the Athenian Acropolis: only pagan gods and their followers can shine forth on the hills of history. Athens progressively triumphs over Jerusalem, in time and on earth.

Van Til is wrong.

In summary:

1. Postmillennialism requires a doctrine of common grace and common curse.

2. The postmillennialist uses the common grace doctrine to provide an explanation for the final rebellion against God at the end of a period of millennial triumph for the kingdom.

3. Satanists need a full manifestation of the kingdom to rebel against at the end of history.

---

36. *Common Grace*, in *Common Grace and the Gospel*, p. 85.

4. They do not "fall from [special] grace" when they rebel.

5. Therefore, as epistemological self-consciousness increases, satanists feel a greater need to rebel.

6. Van Til says that as Christians grow more epistemologically self-conscious and consistent, they lose influence.

7. The unbeliever in fact cannot become fully self-conscious and consistent without committing suicide (Prov. 8:36b).

8. God therefore restrains the full working out in history of the anti-Christian's epistemological self-consciousness until the final rebellion.

9. Satan needs to imitate the church in order to launch an effective attack against the church.

10. Christians can and will become more epistemologically self-conscious.

11. Christians can and will work out the implications of this greater self-knowledge in history.

12. Christians will therefore exercise greater authority over non-Christians, for their worldview is consistent with the creation's law-order.

13. Amillennialists do not believe in long-term visible Christian victory.

14. They do not believe in biblical law as a tool of dominion.

15. If they believed in biblical law as a tool of dominion, they would have to give up their amillennialism.

16. Yet they call on Christians to attempt to fulfill the terms of the dominion covenant ("creation mandate").

17. To be without biblical law is to operate in terms of autonomous, impersonal natural law, or else mysticism (or some combination of the two).

18. Dooyeweerdianism is just such a combination.

19. Premillennialists agree with amillennialists concerning the irrelevance of biblical law today.

6

SUSTAINING COMMON GRACE

Beware that thou forget not the LORD thy God, in keeping his commandments, and his judgments, and his statutes, which I command thee this day. . . . And thou say in thine heart, My power and the might of mine hand hath gotten me this wealth. . . . And it shall be, if thou do at all forget the LORD thy God, and walk after other gods, and serve them, and worship them, I testify against you this day that you shall surely perish (Deut. 8:11, 17, 19).

Here is the paradox of Deuteronomy 8: the blessings of God can lead to the cursings of God. God's gifts can also lead to arrogance and the temptation to think of oneself as autonomous. Autonomy leads to false worship. False worship leads to destruction. Therefore, what appears to be a good thing, wealth, can become a snare and a delusion. A person's or society's preliminary external obedience to biblical law produces benefits that in turn lead to the destruction of that individual or people who were only in external conformity to the law, but not motivated by an inner ethical transformation.

For the unregenerate, the blessings of God become the means of God's judgment against them in history. The external victories of covenant-breakers become a prelude to disaster for them. The prophets warned the victorious invading armies concerning what God would do to them after He had used them as His rod of discipline against Israel (Isa. 13-23; Zeph. 2).

Common Law, Common Curse

The dual relationship between common law and common curse is a necessary backdrop for God's plan of the ages. Take, for example, the curse of Adam. Adam and his heirs are burdened with frail bodies that grow sick and die. Before the flood, there was a much longer life expectancy for mankind. The longest life recorded in the Bible, Methuselah's, Noah's grandfather, was 969 years. Methuselah died in the year that the great flood began.[1] Thus, as far as human life is concerned, the greatest sign of God's

---

1. Methuselah was 969 years old when he died (Gen. 5:27). He was 187 years old when his son Lamech was born (5:25) and 369 years old when Lamech's son Noah was born (5:28-29). Noah was 600 years old at the time of the great flood (7:6). Therefore, from the birth of Noah, when Methuselah was 369, until the flood, 600 years later, Methuselah lived out his years (369 + 600 = 969). The Bible does not say that Methuselah perished in the flood, but only that he died in the year of the flood. This is such a remarkable chronology that the burden of proof is on those who deny the father-to-son relationship in these three generations, arguing instead for an unstated gap in the chronology.

common grace (long life) was given to men just before the greatest removal of common grace recorded
in history (the flood).

This is extremely significant for the thesis of this
book. The *extension of common grace to man* — the external blessings of God that are given to mankind in
general — is a *prelude to a great curse for the unregenerate*.
We read in the eighth chapter of Deuteronomy, as
well as in the twenty-eighth chapter, that men can be
lured into a snare by looking upon the external gifts
from God while forgetting the heavenly source of the
gifts and the *covenantal terms* under which the gifts
were given. The gift of long life was given to mankind in general, not as a sign of God's favor, but as a
prelude to His almost total destruction of the seed of
Adam. Only His special grace to Noah and his family preserved mankind.

Thus, the mere existence of external blessing at
any point in time is not proof of a favorable attitude
toward man on the part of God. In the first stage,
that of *covenantal faithfulness*, God's special grace is extended widely within a culture. The second stage,
that of *external blessings* in response to covenantal
faithfulness, is intended to reinforce men's faith in
the reality and validity of God's covenants (Deut.
8:18). But this second stage can lead to a third stage,
covenantal or ethical *forgetfulness* (Deut. 8:17). The
key fact which must be borne in mind is that this
third stage cannot be distinguished from the second
stage in terms of measurements of the blessings (economic growth indicators, for example). An increase
of external blessings should lead to the positive feed-

back of a faithful culture: victory unto victory. But it can lead to stage three, namely, forgetfulness. This leads to stage four, *destruction* (Deut. 8:19-20). It therefore requires *special* grace to maintain the "faithfulness-blessing-faithfulness-blessing . . ." relationship of positive feedback and compound growth. Nevertheless, common grace plays a definite role in reinforcing men's commitment to the law-order of God.

Everyone in the Hebrew commonwealth, including the stranger who was within the gates, benefitted from Israel's increase in external blessings. Like the increase in crumbs falling from the table of the faithful, so are the external blessings of God to an unregenerate but externally obedient and submissive population during a time of great special grace to the faithful. Therefore, the curse aspect of the "common grace-common curse" relationship can be progressively removed for a time, until at last the unregenerate can stand their external submission no longer, and they rise up in rebellion, despite the threat of the looming curse. During these times of peace, common grace either increases, or else the mere removal of common cursing makes it appear that common grace is increasing. (Better theologians than I am can debate this point.)

The Reinforcement of Special Grace

The fact is, the unregenerate are like Milton's Satan in *Paradise Lost*: they would rather rule in hell than serve in heaven. They would rather destroy the authority of the covenantally faithful than live in a world of blessings and progress. Ethics is ultimately more fundamental than economic self-interest. These people are *envious*; they prefer to pull down those above them, even though they themselves will suffer losses.[2] They hate living under the table of God's people, no matter how many crumbs fall to them.

Without special grace being extended by God — without continual conversions of men — the positive feedback of Deuteronomy 8:18 cannot be maintained. A disastrous reduction of external blessings can be counted on by those who are not regenerate if their numbers and influence are becoming dominant in the community. Sodom is the best example of this process.

Sodom's Salt

Sodom was the most beautiful area of Canaan. When Abraham gave Lot his choice of land, Lot picked Sodom, "for it was well watered every where, before the Lord destroyed Sodom and Gomorrah, even as the garden of the Lord, like the land of Egypt, as thou comest into Zoar" (Gen. 13:10).

The evil men of Sodom lived in the best of Canaan's land. Yet during Lot's generation, God would destroy every trace of Sodom and Gomorrah, burning them with fire from above. What better representation of the last judgment in all the history of man? (The other, as David Chilton demonstrates in

---

2. Helmut Schoeck, *Envy: A Theory of Social Behavior* (New York: Harcourt, Brace & World, [1966] 1970).

Days of Vengeance, was God's destruction of Jerusalem and the temple in 70 A.D.)

Were the Sodomites vessels of wrath? Assuredly. Did God shower them with blessings? Yes. Did God then shower them with fire? Yes. So at the peak of their blessings, they became totally perverse, in every sense of the word. Then God wiped them from the face of the earth and out of history. He cut off their future, their inheritance. Even the productivity of the land was destroyed. This was symbolized by the pillar of salt that Lot's wife became. Salt was used to salt over a productive area, so that it would never grow crops again, and never be a place of shelter. This is why Abimilech salted over Shechem (Jud. 9:45). It is also why God required the priests to salt the first-fruit offering (Lev. 2:13): a symbolism of the permanent "salting" to come in eternity. "For every one shall be salted with fire, and every sacrifice shall be salted with salt" (Mark 9:49). God's fire is the ultimate salt, the final destruction of reprobate man's ability to exercise dominion.

When regenerate Lot, who was the only source of special grace in Sodom, was removed from Sodom, and the unregenerate men who had been set up for destruction by God no longer were protected by Lot's presence among them, *their* crack of doom sounded (Gen. 18, 19). The effects were felt in Lot's family, for his wife looked back and suffered the consequences of her disobedience (19:26), and his daughters committed sin (19:30-38). But it had been Lot's presence among the Sodomites that had held off God's judgment against them (19:21-22).

The same was true of Noah. Until the ark was completed, the world was safe from the great flood. The people seemed to be prospering. Methuselah lived a long life, but after him, the lifespan of mankind steadily declined. Aaron died at age 123 (Num. 33:39). Moses died at age 120 (Deut. 31:2). But this longevity was not normal, even in their day. In a psalm of Moses, he said that "The days of our years are threescore years and ten; and if by reason of strength they be fourscore years, yet is their strength labour and sorrow; for it is soon cut off, and we fly away" (Ps. 90:10).

What has this got to do with common grace? It illustrates the central theme of this book. God grants evil men common grace in the form of external blessings. Then He destroys them. The greater the common grace, the greater their rebellion. The greater their rebellion compared to God's common grace, the greater God's judgment against them. Sodom is the model. They were the chief beneficiaries of God's *increasing* common grace. They then became the chief objects of God's wrath. It appeared that they would be able to exercise increasing dominion; then in the midst of their prosperity, He utterly destroyed them.

First God grants men the *continuity* of His longsuffering common grace. This can go on for several generations. Then He brings the *discontinuity* of His incomparable judgment when men fail to respond in covenantal faith to God's blessings. What we have to say is that common grace increases as history progresses, but this points to the final judgment. When the Sodomites of life, in the midst of their prosperity

and power, attempt to remove the God-fearing
sources of God's special grace from their midst, or
attempt to Sodomize them, they have symbolically
attacked the table of the Lord. God then burns them
with fire. We see this in the AIDS epidemic that will
eliminate most homosexuals before the year 2000. It
will also bankrupt or radically transform all "public"
(socialized) health care facilities. It may even spread
to the general population.[3] God will not be mocked.[4]

---

3. Gene Antonio, *The AIDS Cover-Up* (San Francisco: Igna-
tius Press, 1986).

4. In 1978, the First Orthodox Presbyterian Church of San
Francisco hired as a paid organist a young man who had recently
joined the church. Once on the payroll, he told the pastor that he
was a practicing homosexual. The church fired him because of
this. "On June 14, 1979, the pastor, the congregation, and the
presbytery were sued. The organist had sued on the grounds that
his employment was protected by the city's gay rights ordinance.
Under the direction of constitutional attorney John Whitehead,
the case went to court for summary judgment in March 1980.
The judge ruled in the church's favor, and the full course of the
suit ended by December. The congregation—with the help of
many—defrayed defense costs of $100,000. Since that time the
church has experienced a number of vandalism attacks culminating in an attempt by an arsonist to burn down the building
and the manse." Charles G. Dennison (ed.), *Orthodox Presbyterian
Church, 1936-1986* (Philadelphia: Committee for the Historian of
the Orthodox Presbyterian Church, 1986), p. 191.

They tried to burn God's house; God soon burned them. A
few months later, in 1981, AIDS was first identified as an epidemic
in the United States. (The disease was originally called GRID by
public health officials: Gay Related Immune Deficiency. Pressure from the homosexual community resulted in a change of its
name: Acquired Immune Deficiency Syndrome. Ah, but just
how is it acquired? AIDS is the nation's only politically protected
disease. Judgment is coming.)

Removing Special Grace

The thesis of this book is that the best way to explain common grace is by comparing it to the crumbs that fall to sinners who sit under the table of the Lord.

The key question with respect to the timing of God's judgment against sinners is this: When do they attempt to destroy the table of the Lord? In other words, when do they do their ethically consistent best to kill, remove, or persecute God's church?

God extends grace to them for the sake of His people. He extended an extra century or so to the men of Noah's day, in order to give Noah sufficient time to build the ark. Once a place of refuge was available for Noah, God sent the flood and destroyed all flesh outside the ark.

God made Sodom a lovely land, in order to lure Lot there. Lot served as savor salt to them initially — as a testimony to God's special grace — and then as judgment salt. Lot's testimony of special grace served to condemn the Sodomites. They rejected his testimony, including the testimony of hospitality shown to strangers (angels). Then they attacked God's church — Lot's family — and the angels led Lot, his wife, and two daughters to safety. Then, when God had completely delivered the source of special grace from their clutches, He brought final judgment on them. (Gomorrah was tossed in as a kind of "extra added attraction.") Lot's wife could not resist the spectacular show. She turned and looked. She demonstrated that she was not the salt of salvation. The rule is: either salt or be salted.

The Pharaoh of Joseph's day was made wealthy because he believed Joseph and *obeyed* Joseph. Egypt got wealthy in order to further the plan of God for His people. In the short run, they were fed. In the long run, they were persecuted. In their final run, they spoiled the Egyptians, and their exodus led to the destruction of Egypt's army (and probably their invasion and defeat by the Amalekites).[5]

Another example is His grace to the Canaanites. He allowed them to remain in the land to care for it, not because He favored them, but because He wanted to give them sufficient time to fill up their iniquity (Gen. 15:16). In the actual invasion by the Israelites, which took seven years, He extended some cities extra time so that the beasts would not take over the land while the fighting was going on. But when they fought the Israelites, He destroyed them. The only exception was the Gibeonites, who tricked the Israelites and subordinated themselves to Israel.

When the beneficiaries of common grace attack the source of both common grace and special grace — the church — then they bring God's judgment in history down on their heads. The table of the Lord falls on them. This is the meaning of Revelation 20:8-9. The final judgment is the final collapse of God's table on the reprobate, cursing them for all eternity.

---

5. Immanuel Velikovsky, *Ages in Chaos*, Volume I, *From the Exodus to King Akhnaton* (Garden City, New York: Doubleday, 1952), ch. 2; cf. Gary North, *Moses and Pharaoh: Dominion Religion vs. Power Religion* (Tyler, Texas: Institute for Christian Economics, 1985), Appendix A.

Millennial Blessings

As I pointed out at the beginning of chapter 4, the Book of Isaiah prophesies a future era of the restoration of long life. This external blessing will be given to all men, saints and sinners. It is therefore a sign of extended common grace. It is a gift to mankind in general. Isaiah 65:20 tells us: "There shall be no more thence an infant of days, nor an old man that hath not filled his days: for the child shall die an hundred years old; but the sinner being an hundred years old shall be accursed." The gift of long life shall come, though the sinner's long life has a special curse attached it: long life is simply extra time for him to fill up his days of iniquity and increase his punishment in eternity. Nevertheless, the infants will not die, which is a fulfillment of God's promise to Israel, namely, the absence of miscarriages (Ex. 23:26).

If there is any passage in Scripture that absolutely refutes the amillennial position, it is this one. This is not a prophecy of the New Heavens and New Earth in their post-final-judgment form, but it is a prophecy of the pre-final-judgment manifestation of the preliminary stages of the New Heavens and New Earth — an earnest (down payment) of our expectations. There will still be sinners in this world, and they will receive long life. But to them it will be an ultimate curse, meaning a *special curse*. It will be a special curse to evil-doers, because an exceptionally long life is a common blessing — the reduction of the *common curse*. Again, we need the concept of common grace to give significance to both special grace and common curse. Common grace (reduced common curse) brings special curses to the rebels.

There will be peace on earth extended to men of good will (Luke 2:14). But this means that there will also be peace on earth extended to evil men. Peace is given to the just as a reward for their covenantal faithfulness. It is given to the unregenerate in order to heap coals of fire on their heads.

Final Judgment and Common Grace

An understanding of common grace is essential for an understanding of the final act of human history before the judgment of God. To the extent that this book contributes anything new to Christian theology, it is its contribution to an understanding of the final rebellion of the unregenerate.

The final rebellion has been used by those opposing postmillennialism as final proof that there will be no faith on earth among the masses of men when Christ returns. The devil will be loosed for a little season at the end of time, meaning his power over the nations returns to him in full strength (Rev. 20:3). However, this rebellion is short-lived. He surrounds the holy city (meaning the church of the faithful), only to be cut down in final judgment (Rev. 20:7-15). Therefore, conclude the critics of postmillennialism, there is a resounding negative answer to Christ's question: "Nevertheless when the Son of man cometh, shall he find faith on earth?" (Luke 18:8). Where, then, is the supposed cultural victory before Christ comes in glory, which postmillennialists predict will come?

The doctrine of common grace provides us with

the biblical answer. *God's law is the primary form of common grace.* It is written in the hearts of believers, we read in Hebrews, chapters eight and ten, but the *work* of the law is written in the heart of every man (Rom. 2:14-15). Thus, the work of the law is universal—common. This common access to God's law is mankind's foundation of the fulfilling of the universal dominion covenant to subdue the earth (Gen. 1:28). The command was given to all men through Adam; it was reaffirmed by God with the family of Noah (Gen. 9:1-7). God's promises of external blessings are *conditional* to man's fulfillment of external laws. The reason why men can gain the blessings is because the knowledge of the work of the law is common. This is why there can be outward cooperation between Christians and non-Christians for certain earthly ends.

From time to time, unbelievers are enabled by God to adhere more closely to the work of the law that is written in their hearts. These periods of cultural adherence can last for centuries, at least with respect to some aspects of human culture (the arts, science, philosophy). The Greeks maintained a high level of culture inside the limited confines of the Greek city-states for a few centuries. The Chinese maintained their culture until it grew stagnant, in response to Confucian philosophy, in what we call the Middle Ages. But in the West, the ability of the unregenerate to act in closer conformity to the work of the law written in their hearts has been the result of the historical leadership provided by the cultural triumph of Christianity. In short, *special grace increased in the West, leading to an extension of common grace throughout Western culture.* Economic growth has increased; indeed, the concept of linear, compound growth is unique to the West, and the theological foundations of this belief were laid by the Reformation. Calvin had distinctly postmillennial leanings,[6] although these were partially offset by a degree of amillennial pessimism.[7]

It was during the period 1560-1640 that many of the English Puritans adopted postmillennialism,[8] and this doctrine was fundamental in changing the time perspective of the Puritan merchants who laid the foundations of modern capitalism. Longer life-spans have also appeared in the West, primarily due to the application of technology to living conditions. Applied technology is, in turn, a product of Christianity and especially Protestant Christianity.[9]

In the era prophesied by Isaiah, unbelievers will once again come to know the benefits of God's law. No longer shall they almost totally twist God's reve-

---

6. Greg L. Bahnsen, "The *Prima Facie* Acceptability of Post-millennialism," *Journal of Christian Reconstruction*, III (Winter 1976-77), pp. 69-76.

7. Gary North, "The Economic Thought of Luther and Calvin," *ibid.*, II (Summer 1975), pp. 103-5.

8. James R. Payton, Jr., "The Emergence of Postmillennialism in English Puritanism," *Journal of Christian Reconstruction*, VI (Summer 1979).

9. Robert K. Merton, *Social Theory and Social Structure* (rev. ed.; New York: Free Press of Glencoe, 1957), ch. 18: "Puritanism, Pietism, and Science"; E. L. Hebden Taylor, "The Role of Puritanism-Calvinism in the Rise of Modern Science," *Journal of Christian Reconstruction*, VI (Summer 1979); Charles Dykes, "Medieval Speculation, Puritanism, and Modern Science," *ibid.*

lation to them. *The churl shall no longer be called liberal*
(Isa. 32:5). Law will be respected by unbelievers.
This means that they will turn away from an open,
more consistent worship of the gods of chaos and the
philosophy of ultimate randomness, including evolutionary randomness. They will participate in the external cultural blessings brought to them by the
preaching of the whole counsel of God, including
His law. The earth will be subdued to the glory of
God, including the cultural world. Unbelievers will
fulfill their roles in the achievement of the terms of
the dominion covenant.

This is why a theology that is orthodox must include a doctrine of common grace that is intimately
related to biblical law. Law does not save men's
souls, but *partial obedience to it does save their bodies and
their culture.* Christ is the savior of all, especially those
who are the elect (I Tim. 4:10).

Antinomian Revivalism vs. Reconstruction

The blessings and cultural victory taught by the
Bible (and adequately commented upon by postmillennialists) will not be the products of some form of
pietistic, semi-monastic revivalism. The "merely soteriological" preaching of pietism—the salvation of
souls by special grace—is not sufficient to bring the
victories foretold in the Bible. The whole counsel of
God must and will be preached. This means that the
law of God must and will be preached. The external
blessings will come in response to the covenantal
faithfulness of God's people. The majority of men
will be converted, at least during some periods of

time. The unconverted will not follow their official philosophy of chaos to its logical conclusions, for such a philosophy leads to ultimate impotence. It throws away the tool of reconstruction, biblical law. They want power, not impotence.

The great defect with the postmillennial revival inaugurated by Jonathan Edwards and his followers in the mid-eighteenth century was their neglect of biblical law. They expected to see the blessings of God come as a result of merely soteriological preaching. Look at Edwards' *Treatise on the Religious Affectations*. There is nothing on the law of God or culture. Page after page is filled with the words "sweet" and "sweetness." A diabetic reader is almost risking a relapse by reading this book in one sitting. The words sometimes appear three or four times on a page.[10] And while Edwards was preaching the sweetness of God, Arminian semi-literates were "hot-gospeling" the Holy Commonwealth of Connecticut into political antinomianism.[11] Where sweetness and emo-

---

10. Consider these phrases: "sweet entertainment," "sweet ideas," "sweet and ravishing entertainment," "sweet and admirable manifestations," "glorious doctrines in his eyes, sweet to the taste," "hearts filled with sweetness." All these appear in just two paragraphs: Edwards, *Treatise Concerning the Religious Affectations*, Volume III of *Select Works of Jonathan Edwards* (London: Banner of Truth Trust, 1961), pp. 175-76.

11. On the opposition to Edwards' toleration of revivalism, not from theological liberals but from orthodox Calvinistic pastors, see Richard L. Bushman, *From Puritan to Yankee: Character and the Social Order in Connecticut, 1690-1765* (Cambridge, Massachusetts: Harvard University Press, 1967), Parts 4 and 5. Bushman also explains how the Great Awakening was a disaster for

tional hot flashes are concerned, Calvinistic antinomian preaching is no match for Arminian antinomian sermons.

The "Great Awakening" of the 1700's faded, and
was followed by the Arminian revival of the early
1800's—the "Second Great Awakening"—leaving
emotionally burned-over districts, cults,[12] and the
Unitarian-dominated[13] abolitionist movement[14] as
its devastating legacy. Because the postmillennial
preaching of the Edwardians was culturally antinomian and pietistic, it crippled the remnants of
Calvinistic political order in the New England col-
onies, helping to produce a vacuum that Arminianism and then Unitarianism filled.

Progress culturally, economically, and politically
is intimately linked to the extension and application
of biblical law. The blessings promised in Romans,
chapter eleven, concerning the effects of the promised conversion of Israel (not necessarily the state of
Israel) to the gospel, will be in part the product of

---

the legal remnants of biblical law in the colony of Connecticut.
The political order was forced into theological neutralism, which
in turn aided the rise of Deism and liberalism.

12. Whitney R. Cross, *The Burned-Over District: The Social and
Intellectual History of Enthusiastic Religion in Western New York,
1800-1850* (Ithaca, New York: Cornell University Press, [1950]
1982).

13. Otto Scott, *The Secret Six: John Brown and the Abolitionist
Movement* (New York: Times Books, 1979).

14. Bertram Wyatt-Brown, *Lewis Tappan and the Evangelical
War Against Slavery* (Cleveland, Ohio: The Press of Case Western
Reserve University, 1969).

biblical law.[15] But these blessings do not necessarily include universal regeneration. The blessings only require the extension of Christian culture. For the long-term progress of culture, of course, this increase of common grace (or reduction of the common curse) must be reinforced (rejuvenated and renewed) by special grace — conversions. But the blessings can remain for a generation or more after special grace has been removed, and as far as the ex-

---

15. John Murray's excellent commentary, *The Epistle to the Romans* (Grand Rapids, Michigan: Eerdmans, 1965), contains an extensive analysis of Romans 11, the section dealing with the future conversion of the Jews. Murray stresses that God's regrafting in of Israel leads to covenantal blessings unparalleled in human history. But the Israel referred to in Romans 11, argues Murray, is not national or political Israel, but the natural seed of Abraham. This seems to mean genetic Israel.

A major historical problem appears at this point. There is some evidence (though not conclusive) that the bulk of those known today as Ashkenazi Jews are the heirs of a converted tribe of Turkish people, the Khazars. It is well-known among European history scholars that such a conversion took place around 740 A.D. The Eastern European and Russian Jews may have come from this stock. They have married other Jews, however: the Sephardic or diaspora Jews who fled primarily to western Europe. The Yemenite Jews, who stayed in the land of Palestine, also are descendants of Abraham. The counter-evidence against this thesis of the Khazars as modern Jews is primarily linguistic: Yiddish does not bear traces of any Turkic language. On the kingdom of the Khazars, see Arthur Koestler, *The Thirteenth Tribe: The Khazar Empire and Its Heritage* (New York: Random House, 1976).

If the Israel referred to in Romans 11 is primarily genetic, then it may not be necessary that all Jews be converted. What, then, is the Jew in Romans 11? Covenantal? I wrote to Murray in the late 1960's to get his opinion on the implications of the Khazars for his exegesis of Romans 11, but he did not respond.

ternal benefits can be measured, it will not be possible to tell whether the blessings are part of the *positive feedback program* (Deut. 8:18) or a *prelude to God's judgment* (Deut. 8:19-20). God respects His conditional, external covenants. External conformity to His law gains external blessings. These, in the last analysis (and at the final judgment), produce coals for unregenerate heads.

Conclusion

The law of God is a tool of dominion. There can be no long-term dominion in defiance of it. When men adhere to its principles externally, they receive God's external blessings. This is common grace. Covenant-breakers are blessed because in their external lives, they are not actively breaking the covenant. They live under the shelter of the table of the people of God. They respond in outward obedience to biblical law and/or to the work of the law written in their hearts.

This common grace obedience brings external blessings. It may also bring external influence. These blessings do not point to the salvation of unregenerate people; if anything, they point to their coming destruction, for reprobates always grow arrogant when they receive God's covenantal blessings. This arrogance leads to their external destruction. But for a time, it appears that they are arrogantly dominant, and that there is no covenantal relationship between covenantal faithfulness and covenantal blessings. The third stage of the process of decline—autonomy with blessings (Deut. 8:17)—will eventually be followed by the fourth stage: destruction (Deut. 8:19-20).

This means that special grace alone can preserve the common grace within a culture. The positive feedback between faith and blessings requires additional faith to sustain the growth process. Common grace is not autonomous. The belief that it is autonomous is the sinful conclusion of the unbelievers (Deut. 8:17). Thus, as God's special grace increases over time, we should expect to see His common grace increase, until the day that the unregenerate can stand their submission no longer, and they rebel. As the bread on the table increases, the crumbs under the table increase.

That there will be a final rebellion at the end of the millennium is no testimony against postmillennialism. It is a testimony to the heart of unregenerate men. They will experience the blessings, and they will have in their hands the tools of dominion. They will as always choose the power religion of autonomous man over the dominion religion of subordination before God. They will rebel. But this final rebellion will be cut short by God's final judgment.

The power religion can bring short-term external victory to ethical rebels. The empires of history no doubt subdued the church from time to time. But they do not conquer the church, for it is the bride of Christ. Thus, the fact that the rebels can surround the church in that final rebellion only testifies to the short-term power of the power religionists. This power does not last long. The church is not destroyed. Instead, the power religionists are destroyed.

Any attempt to preach salvation without the law is futile. The law is the basis of affirming the covenant. It is the basis of positive feedback culturally. Those who preach postmillennial victory apart from adherence to the law are simply pietists in disguise, and postmillennial pietism has always fallen into emotionalism, morbid introspection, and cultural defeat. Jonathan Edwards is the classic example. He was not the last Puritan; he was the *destroyer* of the remnant of Puritanism.

In summary:

1. Biblical law is a tool of dominion: a gift from God.

2. External adherence to the law brings external blessings.

3. External blessings tempt evil men to believe that they produced the blessings autonomously.

4. Autonomy leads to destruction by God.

5. The extension of common grace to covenant-breakers leads to their ultimate rebellion and defeat.

6. Common grace requires further extensions of special grace in order to be sustained.

7. Common grace will increase, Isaiah tells us: the re-establishment of very long lives.

8. Common grace will increase, Isaiah says: an increase in epistemological self-consciousness, leading to the proper identification of churls.

9. Peace on earth will come to ethical

rebels, so long as they remain peaceful and subordinate to biblical law.

10. God's law is the primary manifestation of common grace.

11. The work of the law in all men's hearts testifies to this universal aspect of common grace.

12. Preaching that ignores God's law is antinomian and pietistic.

13. Pietism cannot sustain an advancing Christian culture, for it abandons the tool of dominion: biblical law.

14. External blessings apart from repentance are a prelude to covenantal judgment.

7

EPISTEMOLOGICAL
SELF-CONSCIOUSNESS
AND COOPERATION

The vile person shall no more be called liberal, nor the churl said to be bountiful (Isa. 32:5).

What is meant by epistemological self-consciousness? It means a greater understanding over time of what one's presuppositions are, and a greater willingness to put these presuppositions into action. It affects both wheat and tares.

In what ways do the wheat and tares resemble each other? In what ways are they different? The angels of the parable saw the differences immediately. God therefore restrained them from ripping up the tares. He wanted to preserve the historical process of differentiation. Therefore, the full historical development of both wheat and tares is required by God. Clearly, this is a very strong argument against premillennialism.

As the Christians develop to maturity, they become more powerful. This is not a straight-lined development. There are times of locusts and blight and drought, both for Christians and for satanists (humanists).[1] There is ebb and flow, but always there is direction to the movement. There is maturation. For one thing, the church's creeds improve over time. This, in turn, gives Christians cultural power. Is it any wonder that the Westminster Confession of Faith was drawn up at the high point of the Puritans' control of England? Are improvements in the creeds useless culturally? Do improvements in creeds and theological understanding necessarily lead to impotence culturally? Nonsense! It was the Reformation that made possible modern science and technology.

On the other side of the field—indeed, right next to the wheat—self-awareness by unbelievers also increases. But sinners do not always become fully consistent with their philosophy of chaos. The Enlightenment was successful in swallowing up the fruits of the Reformation only to the extent that it was a pale reflection of the Reformation. The Enlightenment's leaders rapidly abandoned the magic-charged, demonically inspired Renaissance worldview.[2] They retained the humanism of a Bruno, but after 1600, the Enlightenment's *open* commitment to the demonic receded. In its place came rationalism, Deism, and the logic of an orderly autonomous

---

1. Gary North, *Unholy Spirits: Occultism and New Age Humanism* (Ft. Worth, Texas: Dominion Press, 1986).
2. On the magic of the early Renaissance, see Frances Yates, *Giordano Bruno and the Hermetic Tradition* (New York: Vintage, [1964] 1969).

world. They used stolen biblical premises, secularized them, and thereby gained power.

This is not to say that the demonic element ever departed from the Enlightenment. On the contrary, it was fundamental to it. James Billington's magnificent history, *Fire in the Minds of Men: Origins of the Revolutionary Faith* (1980), shows that the French Revolution had its origins in occultism and sexual debauchery. The origin of twentieth-century socialism, both Communism and Nazism, was in part the occult underground of the nineteenth century.[3] There is even plausible evidence that Karl Marx had been involved in some sort of demonism as a young man, and perhaps even later.[4] But these occult origins of modern revolutionism and "scientific socialism" were deliberately hidden by their founders, and especially by the guild of professional historians. Billington is a maverick in this respect.[5]

Christians and humanists have borrowed from each other. Isaac Newton was an Arian monotheist,[6] not a trinitarian Christian, although he kept his theological views to himself. His theories of physics were based on his faith in the providential control of all things by God. He even devoted the last decades of his life to a study of the dating of the exodus.

---

3. James Billington, *Fire in the Minds of Men: Origins of the Revolutionary Faith* (New York: Basic Books, 1980).

4. Richard Wurmbrand, *Marx and Satan* (Westchester, Illinois: Crossway, 1986).

5. Gary North, *Conspiracy: A Biblical View* (Westchester, Illinois: Crossway, 1986), ch. 7.

6. Arius was the early fourth-century monotheist who opposed the orthodox trinitarian Athanasius.

Nevertheless, his mathematical formulas could be used, and were used, by anti-Christian thinkers of the Enlightenment to defend the idea of autonomous natural law that governs an autonomous universe.[7] They took his views far down the road toward atheism, which had not been Newton's intent.

So compelling was Newton's vision of mathematically governed reality that Christians like Cotton Mather hailed the new science of Newtonian mechanics as essentially Christian.[8] It was so close to Christian views of God's orderly being and the creation's reflection of His orderliness, that the Christians unhesitatingly embraced the new science. Christians did not see (and still generally have not seen) the danger to their view of the cosmic personalism of the universe[9] that autonomous natural law systems pose.

What we find, then, is that Christians were not fully self-conscious epistemologically, and neither were the pagans. In the time of the apostles, because of the historically unique revelation of God, church leaders enjoyed a high degree of self-awareness. The church's war with Rome helped to maintain this awareness. The church was persecuted, and it won. But even in this era of the Roman Empire, there was considerable muddled thinking on both sides. The attempt, for example, of Julian the Apostate to

---

7. Louis I. Bredvold, *The Brave New World of the Enlightenment* (Ann Arbor: University of Michigan Press, 1961).

8. Cotton Mather, *The Christian Philosopher* (London, 1721).

9. Gary North, *The Dominion Covenant: Genesis* (Tyler, Texas: Institute for Christian Economics, 1982), ch. 1: "Cosmic Personalism."

revive paganism late in the mid-fourth century was ludicrous—it was half-hearted paganism, at best. It failed after two years.

In the middle of the second century, A.D., Marcus Aurelius, a true philosopher-king in the tradition of Plato, had been a major persecutor of Christians; Justin Martyr died during Aurelius' years as emperor. But the emperor's debauched son Commodus was too busy with his 300 female concubines and 300 males[10] to bother about systematic persecutions. Who was more self-conscious, epistemologically speaking? Aurelius still had the light of reason before him; his son was immersed in the religion of revolution and escape—cultural impotence. He was more willing than his philosopher-persecutor father to follow the logic of his satanic faith. He preferred debauchery to power. Commodus was assassinated 13 years after he became Emperor. The Senate resolved that his name be execrated.[11]

The Marxist Challenge

The African tribe, the Ik (see chapter 5), is so consistent with pagan demonism that its members are a threat to no one but themselves. Communists, on the other hand, *are* a threat. They believe in linear history (officially, anyway—their system is at bottom

---

10. Edward Gibbon, *The History of the Decline and Fall of the Roman Empire*, Milman edition, 5 Vols. (Philadelphia: Porter & Coates, [1776]), I, p. 144.

11. Ethelbert Stauffer, *Christ and the Caesars* (Philadelphia: Westminster Press, 1955), p. 223.

cyclical, however[12]). They believe in law. They believe in destiny. They believe in historical meaning. They believe in historical stages, though not ethically determined stages such as we find in Deuteronomy. They believe in science. They believe in literature, propaganda, and the power of the written word. They believe in higher education. In short, Marxists have a philosophy which is a kind of perverse mirror image of Christian orthodoxy. They are dangerous, not because they are acting consistently with their ultimate philosophy of chaos, but because they limit the function of chaos to one area alone: the revolutionary transformation of bourgeois culture. (I am speaking here primarily of Soviet Communists.) But where are they winning converts? In the increasingly impotent, increasingly existentialist, increasingly antinomian West.

Until the West abandoned its remnant of Christian culture, Marxism could flourish only in the underdeveloped, basically pagan areas of the world. An essentially Western philosophy of optimism, Communism found converts among the intellectuals of the Far East, Africa, and Latin America, who saw the fruitlessness of Confucian stagnation and relativism, the impotence of demonic ritual, or the dead-end nature of demon worship. Marxism is powerful only to the extent that it has the trappings of Augustinianism, coupled with subsidies, especially technological subsidies and long-term credit, from Western industry, banks, and governments.

---

12. Gary North, *Marx's Religion of Revolution: The Doctrine of Creative Destruction* (Nutley, New Jersey: Craig Press, 1968), pp. 100-1.

There is irony here. Marx believed that "scientific socialism" would triumph only in those nations that had experienced the full development of capitalism. He believed that in most cases (possibly excepting Russia), rural areas first would have to abandon feudalism and then develop a fully capitalist culture before the socialist revolution would be successful. Yet it was primarily in the rural regions of the world that Marxist ideas and groups were first successful. The industrialized West was still too Christian or too pragmatic (recognizing that "honesty is the best policy") to capitulate to the Marxists, except immediately following a lost war.

Marxists have long dominated the faculties of Latin American universities, but not U.S. universities. In 1964, for example, there were only about half a dozen outspoken Marxist economists teaching in American universities (and possibly as few as one, Stanford's Paul Baran). Since 1965, however, New Left scholars of a Marxist persuasion have become a force to be reckoned with in all the social sciences, including economics.[13] The skepticism, pessimism, relativism, and irrelevance of modern "neutral" humanist education have left faculties without an adequate defense against confident, shrill, vociferous Marxists, primarily young Marxists, who began to appear on the campuses after 1964. Epistemological rot has left the establishment campus liberals with

---

13. Martin Bronfenbrenner, "Radical Economics in America: A 1970 Survey," *Journal of Economic Literature*, VIII (Sept. 1970).

188 DOMINION AND COMMON GRACE

little more than tenure to protect them.[14]

Since 1965, Marxism has made more inroads among the young intellectuals of the industrialized West than at any time since the 1930's—an earlier era of pessimism and skepticism about established values and traditions. Marxists are successful among savages, whether in Africa or at Harvard—epistemological savages. Marxism offers an alternative to despair. It has the trappings of optimism. It has the trappings of Christianity. It is still a nineteenth-century system, drawing on the intellectual capital of a more Christian intellectual universe. These trappings of Christian order are the source of Marxism's influence in an increasingly relativistic world.

It is also significant that as the appeal of Marxism begins to fade, because of the inability of the Communists to hide the economic failures of Communism and the despair it produces, the Marxists have turned to the Bible. The adoption of liberation theology by Latin American Marxists is not simply a tactic based on the Roman Catholic historical roots of the region. It is also an attempt to infuse a sense of religious fervor and morality into a worldview that is dying. Communism's appeal as a comprehensive worldview is increasingly limited. Word has spread concerning the bureaucratization of life it produces. It needs the language of the Bible to empower it.

---

14. Gary North, "The Epistemological Crisis of American Universities," in Gary North (ed.), *Foundations of Christian Scholarship: Essays in the Van Til Perspective* (Vallecito, California: Ross House Books, 1976).

Satan's Final Rebellion

In the last days of this final era in human history, the satanists will still have the trappings of Christian order about them. Satan has to sit on God's lap, so to speak, in order to slap His face—or try to. Satan cannot be consistent to his own philosophy of autonomous order and still be a threat to God. An autonomous order leads to chaos and impotence. He knows that there is no neutral ground in philosophy. He knew Adam and Eve would die spiritually on the day that they ate the fruit. He is a good enough theologian to know that there is one God, and he and his host tremble at the thought (James 2:19).

When demonic men take seriously his lies about the nature of reality, they become impotent, sliding off (or nearly off) God's lap. It is when satanists realize that Satan's official philosophy of chaos and antinomian lawlessness is a *lie* that they become dangerous. (Marxists, once again, are more dangerous to America than are the Ik.) They learn more of the truth, but they pervert it and try to use it against God's people.

Thus, the biblical meaning of epistemological self-consciousness is not that the satanist becomes consistent with Satan's official philosophy (chaos), but rather that Satan's army becomes consistent with what Satan really believes: that order, law, and power are the product of God's hated order. They learn to use law and order to build an army of conquest. In short, *they use common grace*—knowledge of God's truth—*to pervert the truth and to attack God's people*. They turn from a false knowledge offered to them by Satan, and they adopt a perverted form of truth to use in their rebellious plans. They *mature*, in other words. Or, as C. S. Lewis has put into the mouth of his fictitious character, the senior devil Screwtape, when materialists finally believe in Satan but not in God, then the war is over.[15] Not quite; when they believe in God, know He is going to win, and nevertheless strike out in fury — not blind fury, but *fully self-conscious fury* — at the works of God, *then* the war is over.

Cooperation

How, then, can we cooperate with such men? Simply on the basis of common grace. *Common grace has not yet fully developed.* When it does, the covenant-keepers will at last rebel. Until then, we can cooperate with them, but this cooperation must always be in the interests of God's kingdom. The decision as to whether or not a particular *ad hoc* association is beneficial must be made in terms of standards set forth in biblical law. Common grace is not common ground; there is no common ground uniting men except for the image of God in every man. Christians, not pagans, are supposed to set the agenda in any cooperative venture. Pagans sit under the King's table; we do not sit under Satan's. They are supposed to feast on our leftovers, not we on their's.

Because external conformity to the terms of biblical law does produce visibly good results — contrary

---

15. C. S. Lewis, *The Screwtape Letters* (New York: Macmillan, 1969), Letter 7.

to Prof. Kline's theory of God's mysterious will in history—unbelievers for a time are willing to adopt these principles, since they seek the fruits of Christian culture. In short, some ethical satanists respond in external obedience to the knowledge of the work of God's law written in their hearts (Rom. 2:14-15). They have a large degree of knowledge about God's creation, but they are not yet willing to attack His church. They have knowledge through common grace, but they do not yet see what this means for their own actions. (To some extent, the Communists see, but they have not yet followed through; they have not launched a final military assault against the West.)

In short, honesty *really is* the best policy. If Christians are honest, non-Christians will want to cooperate with them. The non-Christian wants the blessings that Christians get through honest labor. Thus, Laban hired Jacob; Potiphar employed Joseph, as did the ruler of the jail and then Pharaoh; the kings of Babylon and Medo-Persia sought Daniel's counsel, etc. They want the fruits of biblical faith, even if they do not want the covenantal roots.

Shared Knowledge

The essence of Adam's rebellion was not intellectual; it was *ethical*. No one has argued this more forcefully than Van Til. The mere addition of knowledge to or by the unregenerate man does not alter the essence of his status before God. He is still a rebel, but he may possess extensive knowledge. Such knowledge can be applied to God's creation, and it will produce beneficial results. Knowledge can also produce a holocaust. *The issue is ethics, not knowledge.* Thus, men can cooperate in terms of mutually shared knowledge; ultimately, they cannot cooperate in terms of a mutually shared ethics. This is why God separates people eternally at the day of final judgment: the development of men's rival ethics over time makes any cooperation impossible. The satanists cannot stand to be in subjection to God, God's law, and God's people. They eventually rebel.

What of the *special curse?* Common grace increases the unregenerate man's special curse. When common grace increases to its maximum, the special curse of God is revealed: total rebellion of man against the *truth* of God and *in terms of His common grace* —knowledge, power, wealth, prestige, etc.—which then leads to final judgment. God does remove part of His restraint at the very end: the restraint on suicidal destruction. He allows them to achieve that death which they love (Prov. 8:36b). But they still have power and wealth right up to the end, as in the Babylonian Empire the night it fell (Dan. 5).

Pagans can teach us about physics, mathematics, chemistry, and many other topics. How is this possible? Because God's common grace to them has increased. They had several centuries of leadership from Christians in the United State, as well as from Enlightenment intellectuals who adopted a philosophy of coherence that at least resembled the Christian doctrine of providence. Humanists cannot hold the culture together in terms of their philosophy of chaos—Satan's official viewpoint—but they still can make important discoveries. They also tax Christians at rates far higher than the tyrannical ten percent that Samuel warned against (I Sam. 8:15, 17). They use stolen capital, in every sense.

Christians Must Set the Agenda

When there is Christian revival and the preaching and widespread application of the whole counsel of God, then Christians can once again take the position of real leadership. The unbelievers also can make contributions to the subduing of the earth because they will be called back to the work of the law written in their hearts. Common grace will increase throughout the world.

During this expansion era, Christians must be extremely careful to watch for signs of ethical deviation from those who seemingly are useful co-workers in the kingdom. There can be cooperation for external goals—the fulfilling of the dominion covenant which was given to all men—but not in the realm of ethics.

We should observe the Soviets to see how *not* to build a society. We must construct counter-measures to their offenses. We must not adopt their view of proletarian ethics, even though their chess players or mathematicians may show us a great deal. The law of God as revealed in the Bible must be dominant, not the work of the law written in the hearts of the unrighteous. The way to cooperate is on the basis of biblical law. The law tells us of the limitations on man. It keeps us *humble before God* and *dominant over nature.* It is our task to determine the accuracy and usefulness of the works of unregenerate men who are exercising their God-given talents, working out their damnation with fear and trembling.

Strangers within the gates were given many of the benefits of common grace — God's response to the conversion of the Hebrews. They received full legal protection in Hebrew courts (Ex. 22:21; 23:9; Deut. 24:17). They were not permitted to eat special holy foods (Ex. 29:33; Lev. 22:10), thereby sealing them off from the religious celebrations of the temple. But they were part of the feast of the tithe, a celebration before the Lord (Deut. 14:22-29). Thus, they were beneficiaries of the civil order that God established for His people. They also could produce goods and services in confidence that the fruits of their labor would not be confiscated from them by a lawless civil government. This made everyone richer, for all men in the community could work out the terms of the dominion covenant.

We are told that the natural man does not receive the things of the Spirit (I Cor. 2:14-16). We are told that God's wisdom is seen as foolishness by the unregenerate (I Cor. 1:18-21). There is an unbridgeable separation philosophically between unbelievers and believers. They begin with different starting points: chaos vs. creation, man vs. God. Only common grace can reduce the conflict *in application* between pagan and Christian philosophy. The ethical rebellion of the unregenerate lies beneath the surface, smoldering, ready to flare up in wrath, but he is restrained by God and God's law. He needs the power that biblical law provides. Therefore, he assents to some of the principles of applied biblical law and conforms himself to part of the work of the law that is written on his heart. But on first principles, he cannot agree. And even near the end of time, when men may confess the existence of one God and tremble at the thought, they will not submit their egos to that God. They will fight to the death—to the second death—to deny the claims that the God of the Bible has over every part of their being.

Thus, there can be cooperation in the subduing of the earth. But Christians must set forth the strategy and the tactics. The unregenerate man will be like a paid consultant; he will provide his talents, but the Lord will build the culture.

Common Grace vs. Common Ground

We must not argue from common grace to common ground philosophical principles, such as the hypothetical "principle of non-contradiction" or an equally hypothetical "natural law." As common grace increases over time, there will be greater and greater separation ethically in the hearts of men. With the increase of common grace, we come closer to that final rebellion in all its satanic might. Common grace combines the efforts of men in the subduing of the earth, but Christians work for the glory of God openly, while the unregenerate work (officially) for the glory of man or the glory of Satan. They do, in fact, work to the glory of God, for on that last day every knee shall bow to Him (Phil. 2:10). The wealth of the wicked is laid up for the just (Prov. 13:22b). But ethically speaking, they are not self-consciously working for the glory of God.

All facts are interpreted facts, and the *interpretation*, not the facts as such—there are no "facts as such" —is what separates the lost from the elect. Inevitably, the natural man holds *back* (actively suppresses) the truth in unrighteousness (Rom. 1:18).[16] No philosophical proofs of God (other than a proof which begins by assuming the existence of the God revealed in the Bible) can link unregenerate minds with regenerate.[17] God the Father, not logic, brings men to a saving knowledge of Jesus Christ (John 6:44). There is no common ground philosophically, only metaphysically. We are made in God's image by a common Creator (Acts 17:24-31). Every man knows this. We can, as men, only remind all men of what they know. God uses this innate knowledge to condemn lawfully all unregenerate men.

The unbeliever uses *stolen intellectual capital* to reason correctly—correctly in the sense of being able to use that knowledge as a tool to subdue the earth, not in the sense of knowing God as an ethically adopted son knows Him (John 1:12). His conclusions can correspond to external reality sufficiently to allow him to work out his rebellious faith to even greater destruction than if he had not had accurate knowledge (Luke 12:47-48). He "knows" somehow that "2 plus 2 equals 4," and also that this fact of mental symmetry can be used to cause desired effects in the

16. Murray, *Romans*, commenting on Romans 1:18.
17. Van Til, *The Defense of the Faith* (Philadelphia: Presbyterian and Reformed, 1963), attacks the traditional Roman Catholic and Arminian proofs of God. They do not prove the God of the Bible, he argues, only a finite god of the human mind.

external realm of nature. Why this mental symmetry should exist, and why it should bear any relation to the external realm of nature, is unexplainable by the knowledge of natural man, a fact admitted by Nobel prize-winning physicist, Eugene Wigner.[18]

Christians, because they have a proper doctrine of creation, can explain the coherence of men's minds, the coherence of the universe, and the coherence of the link between the two. The unbeliever cannot explain this coherence by means of a philosophy of ultimate randomness. Nevertheless, he operates as if he could explain it. He operates in faith. So the unbeliever uses stolen intellectual capital at every step.

Because the unbeliever's capital base is ultimately God's, Christians can use some of his work (by checking his findings against the revelation in the Bible), and the unbeliever can use the work of Christians. The earth will be subdued. The closer the unbeliever's presuppositions are to those revealed in the Bible (such as the conservative economist's assumption of the fact of economic scarcity, corresponding to Genesis 3:17-19), the more likely that the discoveries made in terms of that assumption will be useful. By useful, I mean useful in the

---

18. Eugene Wigner, "The Unreasonable Effectiveness of Mathematics in the Natural Sciences," *Communications on Pure and Applied Mathematics* XIII (1960), pp. 1-14. See also Vern Poythress, "A Biblical View of Mathematics," in Gary North (ed.), *Foundations of Christian Scholarship: Essays in the Van Til Perspective* (Vallecito, California: Ross House, 1976), ch. 9. See also his essay in *The Journal of Christian Reconstruction*, I (Summer 1974).

common task of all men, subduing the earth. Thus, there can be cooperation between Christians and non-Christians.

Conclusion

The Fall of man was ethical, not intellectual. Men's minds are under a curse, for man himself is under a curse, but the problem with man's mind is primarily ethical. Thus, Christians can use the technical skills and specialized knowledge of the unbelievers, just as unbelievers can use the Christian's talents. The division of labor through voluntary market exchange helps each group build up its respective kingdom.

We can cooperate with the enemy in positive projects because of common grace. Our long-term goals will be achieved because we have special grace. We can set the agenda. We have the ethical goods; they have the ethical "bads." They want the benefits of biblical social order. They can be the hewers of wood and drawers of water (Josh. 9) until the day when they at last rebel, and God crushes them for all eternity.

In summary:

1. Both wheat and tares develop to maturity.
2. There is ebb and flow in the expansion of God's visible earthly kingdom.
3. There is creedal progress.
4. Covenant-breakers also develop epistemologically.
5. Power-seekers do not work out in prac-

tice what their increasingly self-conscious suicidal theology leads them toward.

6. Newton's worldview was not consistently anti-trinitarian.

7. Christians adopted Newton's worldview
uncritically.

8. This has led to confusion, as each side
has progressively become more self-conscious.

9. Marcus Aurelius was less consistent with
paganism, and therefore more of a threat to the
church, than his debauched son Commodus.

10. The Marxists are more of a threat to the
West than the African tribe, the Ik.

11. The Marxists have stolen a biblical outlook, so they are more successful in recruiting
despairing savages.

12. Satan dares not become consistent with
his self-professed philosophy of existence if he
wishes to rebel against God in power.

13. The satanists need common grace in
order to run a successful rebellion against God
and God's kingdom.

14. We can cooperate with our ethical enemies because Bible-based conclusions still dominate society.

15. Biblical principles produce benefits that
unbelievers want.

16. They will cooperate with us if they want
more of these benefits, and if we are faithful
servants before God.

17. Christians are to set the agenda for cooperative ventures with pagans. We hire their
services. They sit under the King's table.

18. In the division of labor, pagans do possess valid knowledge that we can use for God's purposes.

19. The guide to proper cooperation is biblical law.

20. Common grace in no way promotes a common ground intellectually.

21. There is no common ground intellectually, except the image of God in all men.

22. Only the doctrine of creation can offer a sufficient reason why man's mind can grasp the laws of nature.

8

FILLED VESSELS

Hath not the potter power over the clay, of the same lump to make one vessel unto honour, and another unto dishonour? What if God, willing to shew his wrath, and to make his power known, endured with much longsuffering the vessels of wrath fitted to destruction; and that he might make known the riches of his glory on the vessels of mercy, which he had afore prepared unto glory, even us, whom he hath called, not of the Jews only, but also of the Gentiles? (Rom. 9:21-24).

God has created two kinds of vessels: vessels made to receive His honor, and vessels made to receive His dishonor. The latter are called vessels of wrath.

The text does not say, nor does Paul's argument warrant, the idea that the vessels were made by God to receive either honor or dishonor, mercy or wrath. They are not "neutral vessels," each awaiting whatever the vessel itself may pour into it in history. The analogy is that of the potter and the clay. "Therefore hath he mercy on whom he will have mercy, and unto whom he will he hardeneth" (v. 18).

Why does he raise the analogy of the potter and the pot? Because it is the next stage in the argument of the self-professed autonomous man against the doctrine of the absolute sovereignty of God in choosing some people to receive eternal life, and others to receive eternal judgment. The autonomous man immediately sees the logical implication of Paul's assertion, and counters with the well-known and traditional argument that this would deny the free will (autonomy) of the individual. "Thou wilt say then unto me, Why doth he yet find fault? For who hath resisted his will?" (v. 19).

Two Kinds of Logic

Paul does not say that this answer is illogical. It is so logical that he asserts, "Thou wilt then say unto me. . . ." He knows just how logical the argument is. He replies instead that the argument is *ethically illegitimate*. "Nay but, O man, who art thou that repliest against God? Shall the thing formed say to him that formed it, Why hast thou made me thus?" (v. 20). He then presents the analogy of the pots and the potter. The potter does what He wants to with the lump of clay. He has a perfect right to make vessels of destruction with it. Asking this question—"Why doth he yet find fault?"—is an act of rebellion. Asserting any variant of it, such as "This makes God the author of sin" is also an act of rebellion, for the Bible says that God is not the author of confusion (I Cor. 14:33), or any other sin.

It is crystal clear what Paul is arguing. The structure of his argument is obvious. God makes two sorts of ethical vessels out of one common clay, humanity. Each type of vessel has its respective eternal destiny. The vessels have no say in the matter. They cannot legitimately reply to the Creator, "Why have you made me thus? And since you have, how can you legitimately hold me responsible for my ethical acts and my eternal destiny?" Why not? Because God *is* the sovereign Creator.

I realize that this argument leaves no room for what is commonly called free will, meaning autonomy, meaning that God either does not control (or may not even know) whether a man will or will not accept His grace in Jesus Christ. On the contrary: God knows, God determines, and God is the sovereign Potter. He predestinates. He chose the redeemed before the foundation of the world. "Blessed be the God and Father of our Lord Jesus Christ, who hath blessed us with all spiritual blessings in heavenly places in Christ; according as he hath chosen us in him before the foundation of the world, that we should be holy and without blame before him in love: having predestinated us unto the adoption of children by Jesus Christ to himself, according to the good pleasure of his will, to the praise of his glory of his grace, wherein he hath made us accepted in the beloved" (Eph. 1:3-6).

Would any reader test himself to see if any traces of humanism remain in his thinking? Here is *the* test. If the theology of Paul in Romans 9 and Ephesians 1 in any way disturbs a person, then there are traces of autonomous (humanist) man still left in his thinking. If any variation of the forbidden argument appears in a person's mind — "Why doth he yet find fault? For who hath resisted his will?" — then he still is thinking humanistically. If he clings to the doctrine of free will because it is a logical corollary of personal responsibility, then he is still thinking rebelliously. He has substituted humanism's logic for the express teaching of Romans 9. Paul makes it clear: (1) complete, eternal responsibility is inescapable, and (2) God predestines some to be vessels of wrath and others to be vessels of His grace. We must affirm both doctrines, not because of their logic or lack of logic, but because of God's explicit revelation in Romans 9. To reject Paul's conclusion is to reject a portion of His inspired Word, which is the essence of humanism and rebellion. It is Adam's sin.

Did you pass the test?

Few Christians do. This is why the doctrine of common grace has gone on in Calvinist circles and not in anti-Calvinist circles. Those who are not Calvinists do not believe in God's double predestination, meaning the *equal ultimacy of wrath and grace.* (For that matter, some Calvinists don't accept it either, which has affected some of the debates over common grace.) The question arises: How does God view those who are not predestined to eternal life? Does He regard them with some degree of favor, or none, during their earthly lives? Do they as "creatures as such" or "men as such" become the recipients of his love or favor, "after a fashion"? Is the unregenerate vessel of wrath in some way the object of God's favor to "clay in general"? The Synod of 1924 said yes. Hoeksema said no. Hoeksema was correct.

Two Kinds of Love

The theological confusion arises because of the conventional definition of love, which is defined as favor or the emotional attachment of one person to another. This is not how the Bible defines love. Love in the Bible comes in two forms, depending on whether a person is a vessel of blessing or a vessel of wrath. There is love with attachment and love without attachment. The first is positive in its emotive attachment and also judicial; the second is negative in its emotional detachment, and also judicial. The first involves *continuity* (inheritance by God's adoption); the second involves *discontinuity* (disinheritance by God's wrath).

For those in God's covenant, love has all five categories of the covenant in the form of blessing: (1) the presence of God the transcendent; (2) hierarchy (a place in God's church); (3) the law of God (law written in the heart); (4) the judgment of God (justification as God's forensic declaration of their righteousness); and (5) inheritance (as adopted sons). Those outside the covenant also have all five points, but in the form of wrath: (1) presence of God as accuser, even in hell (Ps. 139:8); (2) hierarchy (God is sovereign over them); (3) the law of God (the work of the law in the heart); (4) the judgment of God (God's forensic declaration of their guilt); (5) inheritance (from earthly wrath to eternal wrath).

Thus, when God tells us to love our fellow man,

we are to show sinners the same kind of judicial love that God shows them. We are to represent God to them. *First*, we are to serve as accusers, either verbally or by setting a good example. It was David's sin of adultery, Nathan said, which gave the enemies of God an opportunity to blaspheme (II Sam. 12:14). He offered them a poor testimony. God showed His wrath against David to remind the blasphemers of the consequences of sin. God killed the baby (vv. 15-19). *Second*, we are to seek lawful rule over them civilly, in order to bring them under God's hierarchy in civil law. *Third*, we are to preach the law of God to them. This was required every seventh year in Israel (Deut. 31:10-13). *Fourth*, we are to serve as civil judges over them, executing righteous civil judgment. *Fifth*, we are to refrain from coveting their property, for it is the inheritance of their children. We are instead to work hard and inherit that inheritance by our productivity. The wealth of the wicked is laid up for the righteous (Prov. 13:22b).

We are not told to love them indiscriminately. The proper form of love is defined by the covenantal position of love's recipient. We do not love unbelievers as if they were believers. This is why Paul forbade mixed marriages between covenant-keepers and covenant-breakers. To love an unbeliever as one should love a believer is forbidden; in the marriage covenant, it is to be unequally yoked (II Cor. 6:14). This is also true in the church covenant, and is the basis of excommunication. Only in the civil covenant are we legitimately allowed to be unequally yoked in history, but it is our God-assigned task eventually to rule over them, as the Israelites ruled the Gibeonites (Josh. 9). We are not to serve them as hewers of wood or drawers of water, except during periods of God's judgment on us historically because of our prior (and possibly continuing) covenantal unfaithfulness to Him. They are to serve us by obeying biblical law.

Filled to the Brim in History

God told Abraham, "But in the fourth generation they shall come hither again: for the iniquity of the Amorites is not yet full" (Gen. 15:16). The historical development of Canaanite culture still was not complete. Did God hate sin in Abraham's day? Of course. Then why did He give the Canaanites four more generations of sinning? To fill up their cup of iniquity. He gave them more rope to hang themselves with. To use the analogy of Romans 12:20, God gave them more time to heap extra coals of fire on their heads.

I have argued that God's common grace increases over time. I have also argued that sinful man's responsibility before God increases because of this additional common grace. We can see this process in four Old Testament examples: the flood's generation, the Canaanites, the Egyptians, and the Babylonians.

The Flood

Long life was extended to the pre-flood population. Methuselah died at age 969 in the year of the flood. Paul notes that the commandment to honor parents is the first commandment to which a promise

is attached (Eph. 6:2). The specific promise is long
life. Here, above all other promises, is the one that
men universally respect. "O, king, live forever" was
a common expression of homage in the ancient
world (Dan. 2:4; 3:9; 5:10). Clearly, those of the era
before the flood were recipients of lengthening life.
Yet they were progressively evil. God finally stood it
no longer, and He killed them all, and all living animals under their covenantal jurisdiction. He made
one exception: Noah. He placed representative animals under Noah's covenantal jurisdiction. He gave
them life.

Why did God give men increasing common
grace if they were growing more evil? As a way to increase the magnitude of their judgment at the flood.
In this case, it was a question of more water on their
heads—fiery coals came eternally. *When God intends to
bring an end to a covenantally rebellious culture, He first increases their power and might.* This speeds up the process of judgment. They fill up their iniquity faster and
higher. Then He destroys them in a discontinuous
act of judgment.

They had a testimony before them: Noah's life.
They also had another: Noah's slowly growing ark.
They of course had the work of the law in their
hearts, but they also had unique historical testimonies to God's covenantal curses, the testimony of ethics (Noah's righteousness), God's coming judgment
(the ark), and of the end of their inheritance (the
flood that the ark pointed to).

In this instance, the wealth of the wicked was not
laid up for the righteous, except technological knowl-

edge that was passed on through Noah's family. Their external wealth was laid up for destruction, a testimony to all men throughout history concerning the final judgment to come. The flood was as close to ending history as God ever came. He promised never to do it again, until the day of judgment. The rainbow is His covenant sign of this promise (Gen. 9:17).

The Canaanites

This was a culture so perverse that God instructed Joshua to destroy all of them, or at least chase them forever out of the land. God was so serious about this that He said that if they refused to destroy them, He would depart from them (remove His presence: Josh. 7:12). Every man, woman, and child of Jericho was killed, except for Rahab's covenanted household.

Samuel later told Saul to destroy the Amalekites, "and utterly destroy all that they have, and spare them not; but slay both man and woman, infant and suckling, ox and sheep, camel and ass" (I Sam. 15:3). But Saul was greedy — he kept the animals for Israel — and lenient to a "fellow ruler," king Agag. For this, God removed the kingship from Saul (15:11). To emphasize the point, Samuel hacked King Agag to pieces (15:33). Agag was a murderer of women and children, Samuel reminded him; so will his mother be childless. This was also a reminder to Saul that Saul had broken the terms of the covenant; this is what God does to those who break it. This is what "cutting the covenant" means (Gen. 15:9-17).

The Canaanites had received the testimony of Abraham and Isaac. The Philistines' response was to fill up Abraham's water wells with dirt, in a display of envy (Gen. 26:14-15). The Canaanites later came under judgment during the famine that drove Jacob and his family down to Egypt. Then they saw that Jacob's son had become ruler of Egypt and the source of bread for Canaan. Still they did not repent.

Then came the exodus. For a generation, Israel wandered in the wilderness. Canaan grew richer, yet the people of Canaan did not repent. They built houses and planted vineyards, but they would not inherit. God was making an inheritance for His people — "houses full of all good things, which thou filledst not, and wells digged, which thou diggest not, vineyards and olive trees, which thou plantedst not" (Deut. 6:11).

God's common grace was heaping coals of fire on their heads. They continued in their sins, filling up the iniquity of the Amorites. God was also making an inheritance for His people. The wealth of the wicked is laid up for the righteous.

This is why there can be an increase in God's common grace in response to evil man's increasingly evil ways. It is a means of testifying to them of a coming judgment which will be historically total. Their external blessings make them worth destroying. God is going to remove their inheritance and give it to His people. He fills up their vessels with blessings because He is about to break them as vessels of wrath, and pour the wealth into the vessels of honor.

When wealth increases in the face of increasing wickedness, temporal judgment is coming. A transfer of wealth is imminent.

The Egyptians

The Pharaoh of Joseph's day brought himself and his nation under the external terms of the covenant. He did what Joseph told him to do. "Thou shalt be over my house, and according unto thy word shall all my people be ruled; only in the throne will I be greater than thou" (Gen. 42:40). He transferred civil authority to Joseph publicly by giving him his ring and the second chariot (41:42-43). Egypt then got rich.

The judgment of famine stripped the people of Egypt of their land, animals, and freedom. They sold themselves into bondage to the Pharaoh in order to buy food (Gen. 47:13-26). They were still evil, so God sold them into slavery to their god, the Pharaoh. But they survived. God gave them life.

Pharaoh gave the family of Joseph the land of Goshen, the best land of Egypt (Gen. 47:6). This was a testimony to Egypt and Canaan. God rewards His people. The Egyptians did not repent as a nation. They despised shepherds (Gen. 46:34), which was the occupation of the Hebrews. So what was God's judgment against them after Moses fled? He delivered them into the hands of the Amalekites, which conventional historians call the Hyksos, or shepherd kings.[1]

---

1. Immanuel Velikovsky, *Ages in Chaos*, Volume I, *From the Exodus to King Akhnaton* (Garden City, New York: Doubleday, 1952); Gary North, *Moses and Pharaoh: Dominion Religion vs. Power*

Many people did join themselves covenantally to Israel in the years following Joseph. They became Hebrews. There is no other possible explanation for the rapid growth of the Hebrews; it could not have been accomplished by a high birthrate alone.[2] But the nation as a whole remained pagan. This is why there was no covenantally faithful Egyptians remaining in Egypt on the night of the Passover. There was a dead firstborn male in every Egyptian household (Ex. 12:29). The covenant had been eliminated by Moses' day. Yet we know that covenant children do persist. So the covenant of grace had never been established in the first place. Thus, we conclude that faithful societies had to submit to circumcision, just as the Shechemites did (Gen. 34) in order to remain in God's social covenant. If they refused to become circumcised as nations, then individuals of foreign nations had to covenant directly with the Hebrews and become Hebrews (Deut. 23:3).

The Egyptians then placed the Hebrews in bondage. They attempted to destroy the source of special grace in their midst. They were allowed by God to increase their evil. God increased their wealth, so

---

Religion (Tyler, Texas: Institute for Christian Economics, 1985), Appendix A.

2. The reason why not is that growing populations are always characterized by large numbers of children. Yet the number of Hebrews who conquered Canaan, 602,000 men, was almost exactly the number of men who came out at the Exodus. This indicates a stagnant population, and one that had been stagnant for at least a generation before the exodus. Thus, it was converts who added to the population prior to the enslavement. See North, *Moses and Pharaoh*, pp. 22-25.

that the Hebrews could spoil them when the exodus came (Ex. 12:35-36). The wealth of the wicked is laid up for the righteous.

The Babylonians

Nebuchadnezzar learned his lesson after his seven years of bestial behavior. In the eighth year after God struck him with insanity, he was restored (Dan. 4:23, 34). He was converted, and wrote this chapter of the Bible.

King Belshazzar was not so wise. He made a feast, even as the Medo-Persian empire was besieging the gates of the city. At this feast, he committed an act of symbolic theft. He took the golden vessels that had been in the temple, and which had been stored in the treasury of Babylon, and he brought them to the feast. He set them before the thousand lords, and they ate their meal using God's vessels as dinner plates. "In the same hour came forth fingers of a man's hand, and wrote . . ." (Dan. 5:5a).

God had not punished Babylon for stealing the vessels of the temple. This violation of the temple was to teach the Hebrews a lesson: not to put their trust in the temple rather than in God's law. Jeremiah had warned them, "Trust ye not in lying words, saying The temple of the Lord, The temple of the Lord, are these. For if ye thoroughly amend your ways and your doings; if ye thoroughly execute judgment between a man and his neighbour; if ye oppress not the stranger, the fatherless, and the widow, and shed not innocent blood in this place, neither walk after other gods to your hurt: then I will cause you to dwell in this place, in the land that I gave to your fathers, for ever and ever" (Jer. 7:4-7).

God brought them to destruction in one night when they ate from those same vessels. The vessels of dishonor are not entitled to eat from the vessels of honor. It is their place to eat the crumbs that fall from the table of the Lord. By elevating themselves to the table of the Lord symbolically, they were immediately destroyed.

This is what the reprobates do throughout history. They are allowed to eat the crumbs that fall from the Lord's table. Then they become discontented with their position of subservience. They revolt and grab the vessels of honor. They place God's people in bondage, as the Babylonians placed the temple vessels in their treasury. As a judgment of God against His disobedient people, this is permitted for a time. They use God's people for their own purposes, as Laban tried to use Jacob, as Potiphar tried to use Joseph, and as the Egyptians tried to use the Israelites. Then they go too far. Symbolically, they eat off of the sacred vessels. They try to destroy God's people, as the Pharaoh tried to kill the male newborns. Eventually, the continuity of common grace to them is cut short in a mighty display of God's great discontinuity of judgment. The final judgment is the archetype: the end of history, the end of the continuity of common grace.

The prison experience leads to the triumph of the righteous. Jacob in Laban's service led to Jacob's leaving with the best of the flock. Joseph's years in the prison led to his position as second in command in Egypt. Daniel ate vegetables at the king's table in Babylon as a servant, but he later ruled, even on that final night of Babylon (Dan. 5:29). Jesus died on a cross—the ultimate attempt of the wicked to consume God's people—but rose again from the dead to gain absolute power (Matt. 28:18), and then He ascended into heaven (Acts 1:9).

The special curse of prison leads to the special blessing of rulership. Simultaneously, the common grace of power leads the reprobate to exercise that power by imprisoning the faithful. The tables are then turned in a display of God's judgment. The table of the Lord crushes them. Overnight, the righteous gain the inheritance of the wicked.

Conclusion

The increase of common grace accompanies an increase in wickedness during the period in which God fills up the vessels of wrath with their iniquity. He increases their inheritance in order to transfer it to His people during the discontinuity of judgment: judgment unto historical oblivion for the reprobate, and judgment of deliverance for the people of God.

The fact of God's increasing common grace alongside of an increase in wickedness is no problem for the person who understands the relationship between historical continuity and discontinuity. It is only when the extraneous and erroneous idea of God's favor toward the reprobate is brought in that common grace becomes a confusing doctrine.

Then another error is added: the idea that the increasing self-knowledge of the reprobate is accompanied by increasing self-consistency with their own principles of God, man, time, and law. In fact, there is *decreasing* consistency: the reprobate must act in terms of God's law in order to gain power. They do not become consistent and therefore commit immediate suicide individually. Instead, they take steps that lead to God's external destruction of them as a covenantal unit. Their cup of iniquity is filled to the brim. Then God disinherits them publicly, and transfers their wealth to His people.

In summary:

1. God has created two types of vessels: dishonorable and honorable.

2. These vessels are not neutral receptacles.

3. The doctrine of free (autonomous) will is humanistic.

4. There are two kinds of logic: biblical and humanistic.

5. Grace and wrath are equally ultimate.

6. God shows no favor to vessels of wrath.

7. There are two kinds of love that correspond to covenant-keeping and covenant-breaking.

8. One is favorable and one is unfavorable.

9. One gives His people tools, and the other gives the reprobates coals of fire.

10. Christians must use the respective kinds of love in dealing with covenant-keepers and covenant-breakers.

11. Common grace increases over time.

12. Evil men become more covenantally powerful over time if God is setting them up for their public disinheritance.

13. This process is illustrated by the flood, the invasion of Canaan, the time in Egypt, and the time in Babylon.

14. When the vessels of dishonor attempt to eat from the table of special grace by trying to destroy the vessels of honor, then God brings judgment.

9

THE INSIDE MAN

*Now he that betrayed him gave them a sign, say-
ing, Whomsoever I shall kiss, that same is he: hold
him fast. And forthwith he came to Jesus, and said,
Hail, master; and kissed him (Matt. 26:48-49).*

Van Til argues, as I do, that increasingly over
time men become more epistemologically self-conscious. They become more consistent intellectually
with their first principles of life. Christians become
more consistent intellectually with the Bible's view of
life, while non-Christians become more aware of the
differences between their views and the Bible's view.
Van Til assumes that this increasing epistemological self-consciousness results in more consistently
led lives. Christians will live in greater conformity to
the standard of perfection set by Jesus, as the Holy
Spirit guides them into all truth. I agree with Van
Til. But Van Til also argues that non-Christians will
become more consistent in their actions, thereby increasing their power over Christians. I disagree. I

argue that they will not become more consistent in their actions with their underlying intellectual presuppositions, for those presuppositions lead them away from dominion and power and toward death. Thus, for the sake of their underlying *ethical* presupposition — the hatred of God and His people — power-seeking reprobates refuse to live consistently with their anti-Christian philosophies of life. Thus, the ethical impulse is primary, not the intellectual.

This raises a major problem: Where does the reprobate learn more about the hated ethical system of Christianity, so that he can rebel against it more effectively by borrowing from it? There is the testimony of the work of the law in each man's heart (Rom. 2:14-15). But there is also the increasingly visible testimony of Christianity. This assumes that Christianity's influence is spreading and beginning to affect every area of life. Why should it be spreading? Because more Christians are living more consistently with the biblical principles of dominion.

So they have the general testimony of the work of the law in their hearts, plus the specific testimony of the lives and effects of Christians (Deut. 4:5-8). This is the "city on a hill" testimony. Do they have anything else?

Apostates as Antichrists

Ray Sutton has pointed to another important testimony: the presence within the camp of the covenant-breakers of former members of the church. This is the testimony of the apostate. There is a former "inside man" who was close to the church and saw it in action. He knows its strengths and its weaknesses. He then puts this information to work for the devil.

Judas is the best example in New Testament history. He was one of the twelve. He was a thief, and he therefore saw to it that he controlled the disciples' money (John 12:6). He was the organization's treasurer, probably one of the two most important of all organizational posts. John P. Roche, a former Socialist Party worker of the 1930's and an assistant to President Lyndon Johnson in the 1960's, remarks:

> In the 1950s and 1960s friends would call me up as a consultant (unpaid) on whether or not to support some cause which appealed to their sense of social justice. My first question was always, "Who is the executive director?", and my second, "Who is the secretary-treasurer?"[1]

Jesus was obviously a nondescript man in appearance. He could disappear into a hostile crowd and not be located by His enemies (Luke 4:30). The Jewish leaders thought it was worth thirty pieces of silver just to hire an inside man who would recognize Him and identify Him to them.

Judas is only one example. There are many. Satan is the archetype. An angel with access to the court of heaven even after his rebellion (Job 1), he had seen God, but he rebelled. He became the instigator of rebellion among men.

---

1. John P. Roche, *The History and Impact of Marxist-Leninist Organizational Theory* (Washington, D.C.: Institute for Foreign Policy Analysis, 1984), p. 57.

Then came Cain. He was an inside man in every respect: family, church, and civil government. He knew enough about God's required sacrificial system to violate its terms and bring an agricultural offering rather than a blood sacrifice. He slew his brother out of resentment (Gen. 4).

Ham was an inside man who illegally entered his father Noah's tent and saw him naked. He immed ately went to his brothers to tell them what he ha(seen (Gen. 9).

Esau became the father of the Edomites (Edōm = red: Gen. 25:30), also called the Idumeans, who remained Israel's enemy right until the fall of Jerusalem. God hated them from the beginning (Mal. 1:2-3). They were forced to become Jews by the Jewish ruler, John Hrycanus in 129 B.C.[2] In the mid-first century, B.C., an Edomite named Antipater became the supreme power in Israel, and his son Herod became king. Thus began the reversal: the elder brother (Esau) now ruled the younger brother (Jacob). It was the Edomites who first began the slaughter in Jerusalem in 70 A.D., before the Romans sacked the city.[3] The night of the slaughter was the last night that anyone could have fled Jerusalem in safety, just before the invasion began.

---

2. Graetz writes: "The enforced union of the sons of Edom with the sons of Jacob was fraught only with disaster to the latter. It was through the Idumaeans and the Romans that the Hasmonaean dynasty was overthrown and the Judaean state destroyed." Heinrich Graetz, *The History of the Jews*, 6 Vols. (Philadelphia: Jewish Publication Society of America, 1893), II, p. 9.

3. Josephus, *The Wars of the Jews*, IV:v:1-4. Reprinted in David Chilton, *Paradise Restored: A Biblical Theology of Dominion* (Tyler, Texas: Reconstruction Press, 1985), pp. 248-52.

Absalom was an inside man—inside David's family. His advisor Ahithopel the Gilonite had been David's advisor (II Sam. 15:12). Their plans were overthrown because of David's friend Hushai the Archite, who pretended to be a defector, and who gave bad advice to Absalom, which Absalom took despite Ahithopel's pleading (II Sam. 17). Also serving David as his insiders in Absalom's camp were Zadok the priest and Abiathar the priest (15:32-37).

The false prophets who advised the evil kings of Israel and Judah were obviously inside men.

The Jews were a constant source of trouble for the early church. They were close enough to the covenant to understand it. They stoned Stephen. They had Paul imprisoned. They cooperated with the Roman government to suppress the spread of the gospel (Acts 5:24-32).

Apostasy as Rebellion

When Satan goes out to deceive the earth, where will he get his recruits? From inside the church. The inside men and women will supply the troops who will surround the church. Their goal will be to destroy the church. They will have lived inside the covenant community, and they will have learned to hate it. But they will know it well, and know its weaknesses. This is what makes the inside man so dangerous, and why he is important to the opposition.

Because the inside man understands the truth, he can serve as an agent for the forces of Satan. When the orthodox trinitarian faith triumphed in fourth-century Rome, the Arians went out and evangelized the tribes surrounding Rome. Later those tribes conquered Rome militarily.

In modern times, some of the most ferocious opponents of Christianity have been former church members or students in church schools.

In 1729, Jean-Jacques Rousseau began his studies for the priesthood at a Roman Catholic seminary. He was expelled a few months later.[4]

Adam Weishaupt was the founder on May 1 (May Day), 1776, of the revolutionary conspiratorial group, the Illuminati. At the time, he was professor of canon law at the University of Ingolstadt in Bavaria.[5] (May Day, of course, is the traditional celebration day of the ancient chaos religion, when children march around the phallic May pole. It is also the chief day of celebration in the Soviet Union, the day they parade their tanks and missiles in front of the Politburo's reviewing stand. You might imagine that the Soviets would celebrate the October revolution as their number-one memorial day, but they don't. You might also imagine that the Western media would occasionally comment on this seeming oddity. They don't.)

Maximilien Robespierre, the "voice of virtue" who beheaded so many during the reign of terror in 1794, had been a prize-winning graduate of the local church school in Arras, France. In 1775, at the age of 17, he was even selected by the school to give a

---

4. Lester G. Crocker, *Jean-Jacques Rousseau*, 2 Vols. *The Quest (1712-1758)*, I, p. 71.

5. James Billington, *Fire in the Minds of Men: Origins of the Revolutionary Faith* (New York: Basic Books, 1980), p. 94.

welcome speech to King Louis XVI and Marie Antoinette. At Paris, he studied at Louis-le-Grand, a college of the University of Paris. He spent much of his time reading Enlightenment literature. He even visited Rousseau once. The unsuspecting priests awarded him a special donation of 600 livres upon graduation.[6] He was their star student scholar of the classics.

The Communist Counterfeit

Consider the phenomenon of Communism. Karl Marx and Frederick Engels had both been fervent Christians in their teens.[7] Marx was baptized at age six in 1824 and confirmed a decade later.[8] At age sixteen he wrote an essay, "On the Union of the Faithful with Christ. . . ." In it, he affirmed: ". . . the history of peoples teaches us the necessity of our union with Christ." "And where is there expressed more clearly this necessity for union with Christ than in the beautiful parable of the Vine and the Branches, where He calls Himself the Vine and calls us the Branches." "Who would not willingly endure sorrows when he knows that through his continuing in Christ, through his works God himself is exalted, and his own fulfillment raises up the Lord of Creation? (John XV, 8)."[9]

---

6. Otto Scott, *Robespierre: The Voice of Virtue* (New York: Mason & Lipscomb, 1974), pp. 18-19.

7. Richard Wurmbrand, *Marx and Satan* (Westchester, Illinois: Crossway, 1986), chaps. 1, 3.

8. Robert Payne (ed.), *The Unknown Karl Marx* (New York: New York University Press, 1971), p. 33.

9. *Ibid.*, pp. 40, 41, 43.

Within three years, he had rejected Christ and had become the enemy of God. He wrote a short, pathetically boring play in imitation of Shakespeare, called *Oulanem*, an anagram for Manuelo = Immanuel = God. Its characters are Lucindo (lux = light) and Pertini (from *perire* = to perish).[10] Oulanem says:

Ruined! Ruined! My time has clean run out!
The clock has stopped, the pygmy house has
    crumbled,
Soon I shall embrace Eternity to my breast, and
    soon
I shall howl gigantic curses on mankind.
Ha! Eternity! She is our eternal grief.
An indescribable and immeasurable Death,
Vile artificiality conceived to scorn us,
Ourselves being clockwork, blindly mechanical,
Made to be fool-calendars of Time and Space,
Having no purpose save to happen, to be ruined,
So that there shall be something to ruin. . . .

Perished, with no existence — that would be
    really living!
While swinging high within the stream of eternity,
We roar our melancholy hymns to the Creator
With scorn on our brows! Shall the sun ever burn
    it away?
Presumptuous curses from excommunicate souls!
Eyes that annihilate with poisoned glances
Gleam exultantly, the leaden world holds us fast.
And we are chained, shattered, empty, frightened,

---

10. *Ibid.*, p. 63.

Eternally chained to this marble rock of Being,
Chained, eternally chained, eternally.
And the worlds drag us with them in their rounds,
Howling their songs of death, and we—
We are the apes of a cold God.[11]

It is obvious that he had left the faith. It is
equally obvious that he was haunted by the eternal
consequences of becoming an excommunicate in a
world that passes into eternity. "Chained, eternally
chained, eternally." He had been an inside man.
And when he rebelled, he did so in the name of the
religion of revolution, that ancient enemy of biblical
religion.[12]

Joseph Stalin had been a seminary student in his
youth.[13] He spent much of his time reading forbidden books: Darwinian biology, Gogol, Chekhov.
One of his schoolmates recalls: "We would sometimes read in chapel during service, hiding the book
under the pews. Of course, we had to be extremely
careful not to get caught by the masters. Books were
Joseph's inseparable friends; he would not part with
them even at meal times."[14]

The vision of Western millennial hope motivated
the Chinese Communists,[15] a vision that sprang

---

11. *Ibid.*, pp. 81-83.
12. Gary North, *Marx's Religion of Revolution: The Doctrine of
Creative Destruction* (Nutley, New Jersey: Craig Press, 1968).
13. Isaac Deutscher, *Stalin: A Political Biography* (New York:
Vintage, [1949] 1962), p. 17.
14. *Ibid.*, p. 17.
15. Seung Ik Lee, The New China: An Eastern Vision of Mes-
sianic Hope (Ph.D. dissertation, University of Pittsburgh, 1982).

from Christian theology originally, and was filtered
through the heretical revolutionary sects of the Middle Ages.[16] Mission schools educated numerous
Chinese converts to Marxism, as well as future black
African Marxists.

The Four Points

Communist theory possesses all four of the most
prominent features of future-oriented Christianity.
Christianity offers a four-point system of progress,
providence (cosmic personalism), ethics (biblical
law), and the self-attesting truth of the Bible.[17] Communists imitate this system and thereby gain the
minds of men who seek relief from the cursed world
of sin.

First, they have a doctrine of *progress*. The hope
of man is in the successful revolution. The proletar-
iat will be triumphant in history. Those who ally
themselves with Communism, the one true representative of the proletarian revolutionary future,
have allied themselves with victory.

Second, they have a doctrine of *providence*. This
providence is impersonal, unlike Christianity's providence of God. The Marxist providence is historical,
the dialectical process. The laws of dialectical history

---

16. Norman Cohn, *The Pursuit of the Millennium: Revolutionary
messianism in medieval and Reformation Europe and its bearing on modern
totalitarian movements* (2nd ed.; New York: Harper Torchbook,
1961); Igor Shafarevich, *The Socialist Phenomenon* (New York: Harper & Row, [1975] 1980), ch. 2.

17. Gary North and David Chilton, "Apologetics and Strategy," *Christianity and Civilization*, 3 (1983).

sustain history. A knowledge of these laws gives to the scientific socialist a theoretical understanding necessary to well-timed, historically significant revolutionary practice. This is a doctrine of *predestination*, which undergirds their hope in the future. There is no escape from the materialist forces of history. Each stage in historical development is inevitable. The mode of production creates its appropriate thought forms, and it also creates the seeds of the next revolutionary transformation.

Third, they have a doctrine of *ethical law*. Each stage of historical development produces its appropriate ethics and philosophy. Since the proletarian state of Communism is the final stage, proletarian ethics is also final. Since this is the final ethical system, it is ultimate. Proletarian ethics is the ethics of the future, but therefore the ethics of the revolutionary present, a tool of social transformation.

Fourth, they have a doctrine of a self-authenticating philosophy. Since all philosophy in the Marxist view is really the ideology of class interests — a theoretical superstructure built on the substructure of the mode of production — then the only final philosophy or final truth is that truth which is built on the proletarian class. Thus, Marxism does not need to appeal to a common-ground philosophy of being. There is no common ground; there is no common being; there is only *becoming* — revolutionary action (praxis) —*until* the victory of the proletarians. Then class warfare ends, and philosophy therefore settles down into permanent truths.

Because Communist theory can offer this comprehensive vision of secular salvation for society, it can compete successfully with Christianity, especially the escapist versions of Christianity. The Communist liberation theologian José Miranda is self-conscious about the ineffectiveness of escapist Christianity:

> Now, the Matthean expression "the kingdom of the heavens" was the only one serving the escapist theologians as pretext for maintaining that the kingdom was to be realized in the other world. Not even texts about glory or entering into glory provided them any support, for the Psalms explicitly teach, "Salvation surrounds those who fear him, so that the glory will dwell in our land" (Ps. 85:10).[18]
>
> Hence what paradise might be, or being with Christ, or Abraham's bosom, or the heavenly treasure, is a question we could well leave aside, because what matters to us is the definitive kingdom, which constitutes the central content of the message of Jesus. The escapists can have paradise.[19]
>
> To speak of a kingdom of God in the other world is not only to found a new religion without any relationship with the teaching of Christ (for none of the texts wielded by escapist theology mentions the kingdom); it is to assert exactly the contrary of what Christ teaches: "The

18. José Miranda, *Communism in the Bible* (Maryknoll, New York: Orbis Books, 1982), p. 14.

19. *Ibid.*, p. 15.

kingdom has come unto you," and "Your kingdom come." The fact that tradition has taught for centuries that the kingdom is in the other world only demonstrates that that tradition betrayed Jesus and founded another religion entirely different.[20]

The enormous appeal of liberation theology in Latin America (and on seminary campuses in the United States) stems from its ability to transfer powerful concepts of the Bible to the revolutionary Marxist vision. Miranda is correct about the otherworldly emphasis of the escapist fundamentalist and traditional religion. He is incorrect about the supposed communism of the gospel. But it takes a degree of theological sophistication uncommon in Christian circles to pinpoint his errors and overcome them by an appeal to the Bible, without also destroying the foundation of the escapist versions of Christianity. Thus, the challenge of liberation theology goes unanswered by those who have the best alternative in their hands (the Bible) but who do not understand what it says about the kingdom of God on earth and in history.

The Apostate as Transmission Belt
The Bible describes the fate of the apostates who have been inside the faith and have left:

For it is impossible for those who were once

---

20. *Ibid.*, p. 17.

enlightened, and have tasted of the heavenly gift, and were made partakers of the Holy Ghost, And have tasted the good word of God, and the powers of the world to come, If they shall fall away, to renew them again unto repentance; seeing they crucify to themselves the Son of God afresh, and put him to an open shame (Heb. 6:4-6).

This probably refers to the Jews of the period between Christ's death, resurrection, and ascension and the fall of Jerusalem in A.D. 70. But its description of the "inside men" of fallen Israel provides us with an understanding of just what they have forfeited and why they are the great enemies of the church. They seek to crucify Christ afresh.

When these people leave the faith, they seek self-justification. They also seek revenge against the gospel message they have rejected and those who preach it still. They take to the enemies of God an understanding of Christianity's vision of victory. They have again and again imparted remnants of this vision and its motivating power to those who were never inside the covenant.

We think of Islam. It, too, has the shadows of the four points. For predestination they substitute fatalism. For a coming spiritual kingdom on earth they substitute military conquest and (in Iran today) revolution. For biblical law they substitute Khadi justice—the law of the mullahs, God speaking to them directly in the midst of changing historical circumstances. But this law is uniquely Islamic law, anti-

Western, anti-rational. For the self-attesting Bible they substitute a self-attesting Koran. Thus, they have also become historically victorious rivals to Christianity.

The apostate serves as a transmission belt of power. He takes Christianity's religion of dominion and implants it into an anti-Christian religious framework. This Bible-influenced substitute becomes a satanic power-seeking religion. These hybrid religions are the transformed heirs of animist, localist, minimal dominion cultures. The escapist religions of individual meditation techniques, or family-bound ancestor worship, or nature worship, or good manners, or monastic isolation, or monkish begging are transformed into pseudo-Christian religions.

Thus, the apostate serves as a pseudo-messiah. He is the motivator. He brings a corrupt gospel to those who otherwise might never be motivated to any victory beyond keeping a hearth fire burning.

The Pre-Christian Spread of the Gospel

The history books have covered up one of the most important facts of history: the worldwide trading patterns of ancient civilization. The operating presupposition of modern historiography is Darwinism. Historians assume that with only a few *local* exceptions, most notably regional empires, man's history has been *evolutionary*. Occasionally, we find a regional empire that somehow constructed progressive alternatives, but these empires always fell or stagnated. Only with modern man have we come to a knowledge of the forces of evolutionary progress, and only we have been able to use science to transform our environment on a systematic, long-term basis.

What would the historian do with evidence that a thousand years before Christ, Celtic missionaries were operating in northern California and British Columbia? What would they do with evidence that in the time of the Judges, or at the latest in the time of Isaiah, Jews had communicated with New Mexican Indians and had left a stone with the ten commandments written in a Canaanitic alphabet (Phoenician or early Hebrew)? What would they do with evidence that as early as the days of Abraham, traders from Scandinavia were operating in what is now Ontario, Canada? We know what they would do, for they have done it. They would heap ridicule on the man and his followers who would dare to present the evidence. The man's name is Barry Fell, a retired Harvard oceanographer and self-taught master linguist. His books contain incontrovertible evidence of a worldwide trading civilization in which religious and cultural groups of many sorts were spanning the globe in search of profitable trades and religious converts.[21] Thus, the idea that the ancient world had never heard of Israel is exaggerated, at best.

To what extent the message of God, God's law, and the restoration of all things actually penetrated ancient cultures is unknown. The work of the law

---

21. Barry Fell, *Bronze Age America* (Boston: Little, Brown, 1982); *Saga America* (New York: Times Books, 1980); *America* B.C. (Chicago: Quadrangle, 1976). Fell's disciples publish a journal, *The Journal of the Epigraphic Society.*

written in men's hearts is a sufficient explanation of many of the parallel myths in ancient societies. But as time goes on, the increasing epistemological self-consciousness of men leads to an increasing rivalry between power-seeking empires and biblical civilization. In our day, the chief rivals are unquestionably epistemological first-cousins of Christianity.

Conclusion

As men seek power without God, they must abandon the animism of the past and the nihilism of the escapist present. They must avoid becoming intellectually consistent with their own religious presuppositions. They must instead be infused with a future-oriented, law-governed, highly disciplined alternative to Christianity. The inside man is the agent of this infusion.

In summary:

1. Men's epistemological self-consciousness increases over time.

2. Christians become more ethically self-conscious as they become epistemologically self-conscious.

3. Unbelievers become less ethically self-conscious as they become more epistemologically self-conscious.

4. The goal of power is attainable only by external obedience to fundamental principles of biblical law.

5. The self-consistency of Christian ethics and Christian philosophy leads to a spread of Christianity's influence.

6. Unbelievers learn from apostates concerning the techniques of dominion, which then become power religions.

7. The apostate become change agents in Satan's kingdom.

8. Examples are Cain, Ham, Esau, Absalom, Ahithopel, false priests, Judas, and the Jews of Jesus' day.

9. On the last day, Satan will recruit his troops from inside the church.

10. Historically, some of the most effective opponents of Christianity have been former Christians.

11. Examples are Rousseau, Robespierre, Weishaupt, Marx, Engels, and Stalin.

12. Communism steals Christianity's four points of civilization building: providence, earthly optimism, law as a tool of dominion, and the self-attesting revelation of God.

13. Islam also steals these same four points.

14. Ancient cultures were in contact with Israel.

15. The apostate serves as a pseudo-messiah.

CONCLUSION

For whom he did foreknow, he also did predestinate, to be conformed to the image of his son, that he might be the firstborn among many brethren (Romans 8:29).

And be not conformed to this world: but be ye transformed by the renewing of your mind, that ye may prove what is the good, and acceptable, and perfect, will of God (Rom. 12:2).

Be ye followers [imitators — NASB] of me, even as I also am of Christ (I Cor. 11:1).

The Christian is called to *ethical self-consciousness.* Out of this comes epistemological self-consciousness. Ethics is the fundamental issue, not philosophical knowledge.

The increase in the ethical understanding of Christians results in their increasing understanding of the Bible's principles of knowledge. Christians think God's thoughts after Him, as creatures made in His image.

For though we walk in the flesh, we do not
war after the flesh: (for the weapons of our warfare are not carnal, but mighty through God to
the pulling down of strong holds;) casting down
imaginations and every high thing that exalteth
itself against the knowledge of God, and bringing into captivity every thought to the obedience of Christ (II Cor. 10:3-5).

The issue is *obedience*, not philosophical rigor.
Obedience in the long run is what brings the church
increasing wisdom and increasing philosophical
rigor.

The followers of Satan cannot expect to match the
church intellectually in the long run, for Christians
have the mind of Christ ethically (I Cor. 2:16). As
Van Til once (or more) said, it does no good to
sharpen a buzz saw that is set at the wrong angle; no
matter how sharp it becomes, it will not cut straight.
So is the mind of man.

The only thing that keeps the covenant-breaker
from going mad and committing suicide is that God
restrains his ability to follow the logic of his anti-God
presuppositions. He also restrains their suicidal im-
pulses. He does this for the sake of His people, who
in history need the cooperation and added productivity of the unregenerate. God restrains them simply to make them productive. Without God's
restraint, they would be impotent.

This is why the kingdom of God will win in any
open competitive contest with Satan's rival kingdoms. Christians unfortunately do not believe this in

our era, which is why they are so fearful. They see the satanic world system getting worse, evil getting richer, and Christian influence declining. The kingdom of righteousness in their view cannot survive a fair fight, let alone an unfair fight. They conclude that God's people are doomed to be historical losers.

Abandoning Responsibility

They simultaneously believe that since Christians cannot win in open competition — socially, intellectually, culturally, economically — any attempt to establish biblical law as the foundation of law and order must be the recommendation of potential tyrants. "After all, if these people are really trying to build a self-consciously Christian society, and if they really expect to win, then they must be planning to impose tyrannical force. We know that Christianity cannot defeat the power religion. Therefore, any program that proposes such a victory must have as its hidden agenda a rival program of power."

Christians have generally accepted as valid the worldview of the power religion. They have concluded that power, and only power, is the basis of successful political programs. They have accepted Mao's dictum that power (and everything else) grows out of the barrel of a gun. They do not accept the operating principle of the dominion religion, namely, that long-term authority is the product of a bottom-up extension of God's strategy of dominion, beginning with self-government under biblical law. They do not believe that biblical law produces social peace and prosperity. Thus, fearing the responsibilities of dominion because they mistake dominion for tyrannical power, and because they do not want to be labeled *Christian* tyrants, Christians seek an alliance with humanistic power religionists against the dominion religion. (A minority of Christians may occasionally seek to become powerful themselves in terms of humanism's acceptable political strategies.)

Christians generally do not believe that God in His providence designed the mind of man for the purpose of man's taking dominion. They do not believe that regenerate minds that necessarily possess the mind of Christ (I Cor. 2:16) are dominically superior to unregenerate minds that have the mind of Satan. Thus, Christians have retreated time and again in the cultural and intellectual battles. They have justified these repeated retreats by devising eschatologies of inevitable, guaranteed defeat for the visible kingdom of God. This makes it easier to run up the white flag. "What else could we expect but defeat? After all, we're Christians."

Our enemies have stolen the Bible's vision of victory and its doctrine of providence. They have reworked these doctrines to fit their requirements. Christians are fearful of an enemy army that has stolen everything positive that it has in its arsenal. Christians do not see that it is our God who makes the rules. In contrast, our enemy knows what wins. Satan cannot win if his followers cling to his own doctrine of chaos. This is why he has stolen our vision and worldview.

Who has the right to adopt such a program of victory? Whose Commander gave a death blow to

His rival's head (Gen. 3:15) at Calvary? Admittedly, the church suffers from a limp, just as Jacob did (Gen. 32:25). The church's heel is injured, just as God promised that Christ's would be (Gen. 3:15). But the enemy's head is crushed. When going into battle, which wound would you prefer to march in with?

Unbelievers appear to be culturally dominant today. Christians have for too long seen themselves as the dogs sitting beneath the humanists' tables, hoping for an occasional scrap of unenriched white bread to fall their way. They have begged humanistic college accreditation associations to certify the academic acceptability of their struggling little colleges. They worry about their own competence. They think of themselves as second-class citizens.

And the humanists, having spotted this self-imposed "second-class citizen" mentality, have taken advantage of it. They have sent Christians to the back of the bus.

Pietism's Retreat

Believers have for over a century retreated into antinomian pietism and pessimism. This retreat began in the 1870's.[1] They have lost the vision of victory which once motivated Christians to evangelize and then take over the Roman Empire. They have abandoned faith in one or more of the four features of Christian social philosophy that make progress possible: (1) the dynamic of *eschatological optimism*, (2)

---

1. George Marsden, *Fundamentalism and American Culture: The Shaping of Twentieth-Century Evangelicalism, 1870-1925* (New York: Oxford University Press, 1980).

the tool of the dominion covenant, *biblical law*, (3) the predestinating providence of God, and (4) biblical presuppositionalism—the self-attesting truth of an infallible Bible.[2] We should conclude, then, that either the dissolution of culture is at hand (for the common grace of the unregenerate cannot long be sustained without leadership in the realm of culture from the regenerate), or else the regenerate must regain sight of their lost theological heritage: post-millennialism and biblical law.

For common grace to continue, and for external cooperation between believers and unbelievers to be fruitful or even possible, Christians must call the external culture's guidelines back to God's revealed law. They must regain the leadership they forfeited when they adopted as Christian the speculations of self-proclaimed "reasonable" apostates. If this is not done, then we will slide back once more, until the unbelievers at last resemble the Ik, and the Christians can begin the process of cultural domination once more. For common grace to continue to increase, it must be sustained by special grace. Either unbelievers will be converted, or leadership will flow back toward the Christians. If neither happens, society will return eventually to barbarism.

Understandably, I pray for the regeneration of the ungodly *and* the rediscovery of biblical law and accurate biblical eschatology on the part of present Christians and future converts. Whether we will see such a revival in our day is unknown to me. There

---

2. Gary North and David Chilton, "Apologetics and Strategy," *Christianity and Civilization*, 3 (1983), pp. 107-16.

are reasons to believe that it can and will happen.[3]
There are also reasons to doubt such optimism. The
Lord knows.

We must abandon antinomianism and eschatologies that are inherently antinomian. We must call
men back to faith in the God of the whole Bible. We
must affirm that in the plan of God there will come a
day of increased self-awareness, when men will call
churls churlish and liberal men gracious (Isa. 32).
This will be a day of great external blessings—the
greatest in history. Long ages of such self-awareness
unfold before us. And at the end of time comes a generation of rebels who know churls from liberals and
strike out against the godly. They will lose the war.

Common Grace Is Future Grace

Therefore, *common grace* is essentially *future grace*.
There is an ebb and flow of both common grace and
special grace throughout history, but essentially the
manifestation of all grace is in the future. It must not
be seen as essentially prior or earlier grace. Only
amillennialists can consistently hold to such a position—antinomian amillennialists at that. Premillennialists at least have the millennium in front of them.
In the amillennial scheme, the final judgment appears at the end of time against the backdrop of
declining common grace. The postmillennial view
sees this final satanic rebellion against a background
of maximum common grace. The *common curse* will

---

3. Gary North, *The Sinai Strategy: Economics and the Ten Commandments* (Tyler, Texas: Institute for Christian Economics,
1986), pp. 86-92: "The Sabbath Millennium."

be at its *lowest* point, the prelude to *special cursing* of eternal duration. The final judgment comes, just as the great flood came, against a background of God's widespread external benefits to mankind in general. The iniquity of the New Testament Amorites will at last be full.

Does the postmillennialist believe that there will be faith in general on earth when Christ appears? Not if he understands the implications of the doctrine of common grace: it leads to a final rebellion by covenant-breakers. Does he expect the whole earth to be destroyed by the unbelieving rebels before Christ strikes them dead—doubly dead? No. The judgment comes before they can achieve their evil goal.

Will God destroy His *preliminary down payment* (preliminary manifestation) of the New Heavens and the New Earth? Will God erase the sign that His Word has been obeyed in history, that the dominion covenant has been nearly fulfilled by regenerate people? Will Satan, that great destroyer, have the joy of seeing God's Word thwarted, His church's handiwork torn down by Satan's very hordes? The amillennialist answers yes. The postmillennialist must deny it with all his strength.

Common grace is extended to allow unbelievers to fill up their cup of wrath. They are vessels of wrath. Therefore, the fulfilling of the terms of the dominion covenant through common grace is the final step in the process of filling up these vessels of wrath. The vessels of grace, believers, will also be filled. Everything will be historically full.

There is continuity in life, despite discontinuities. The wealth of the sinner is laid up for the just. Satan would like to burn God's field, but he cannot. The tares and wheat grow to maturity, and then the reapers go out to harvest the wheat, cutting away the chaff and tossing it into the fire. Satan would like to turn back the crack of doom, return to ground zero, return to the garden of Eden, when the dominion covenant was first given. He cannot do this. History moves forward toward the fulfillment of the dominion covenant (Gen. 1:28)—as much a fulfillment as pre-final-judgment mankind can achieve. At that point, common grace produces malevolence—absolutely and finally malevolence—when Satan uses the last of his time and the last of his power to strike out against God's people. When he uses his gifts to become finally, totally destructive, he is cut down from above. *This final culmination of common grace is Satan's crack of doom.*

And the meek—meek before God, active toward His creation—shall at last inherit the earth. A renewed earth and renewed heaven is the final payment by God the Father to His Son and to those He has given to His Son. This is the postmillennial hope.

Answers

In the Introduction to this book, I asked a series of questions. Let me summarize my answers.

Does a gift from God imply His favor?

No. A gift from God is given to unbelievers for two primary reasons: to bring them to humble, grateful repentance, and to heap coals of fire on the heads of those who refuse to repent (Rom. 12:20). There is no favor shown to the latter group.

Gifts to the unregenerate also extend the division of labor and thereby increase benefits for Christians. Christians can work for, with, or over unbelievers who at least to some degree manifest external righteousness. This enables everyone to increase his own output.

Does an unregenerate man possess the power to do good?

Yes. The unregenerate man has the work of the law written on his heart (Rom. 2:14-15). God grants him the power to perform externally righteous acts. This is an aspect of God's common grace to mankind. Man cannot do enough good to earn his way to heaven, but God enables him to do enough good to distinguish himself in time and eternity from even more systematically perverse people (Luke 12:47-48).

Does the existence of good behavior on the part of the unbeliever deny the doctrine of total depravity?

No. The depravity of man is total *in principle*. It is not total *in history*. If it were, sinners could not live. God, because of Christ's sacrifice on the cross, withholds His absolute, final judgment until the last day. This gives all men temporal life for a time.

God restrains the sinfulness of man because He shows common grace to all men and special grace to some men. He does not allow anyone to work entirely consistently with evil presuppositions. Though mankind rebelled definitively in the garden, God actively restrains the progressive increase of sinful behavior of individuals and cultures in history.

Does history reveal a progressive separation between saved and lost?

Yes, but this separation is ethical, not metaphysical. Those within the kingdom of God grow more self-consistent with God's ethical requirements. They become imitators of Christ, conforming themselves to His law, so that they may progressively reveal themselves as His people. They imitate His perfect humanity (though never His divinity).

God restrains the covenant-breakers from becoming totally consistent with their own God-defying presuppositions until the final rebellion just before the final judgment. Prior to this final judgment, we should expect to see covenant-breakers act more in conformity with God's external laws, so that they can participate in the external covenantal blessings.

The separation is therefore primarily internal and ethical, as time goes on. To the extent that covenant-breakers externalize their defiance against God, they will be rendered increasingly impotent: drug addiction, disease, military defeat, and all the other curses listed in Deuteronomy 28:15-68.

Would such a separation necessarily lead to the triumph of the unregenerate?

No; just the opposite. The ethical separation of covenant-breakers from God is repressed by those covenant-breakers who wish to prosper. Those who refuse to exercise self-restraint (under God's common grace) are steadily eliminated from places of influence and power.

Is there a common ground intellectually between Christians and non-Christians?

No. The only common ground between the saved and the lost is the image of God in all men. Any attempt to find a common approach to reason is fruitless. The unbeliever begins with the assumption of his own sovereignty before God. The believer is required to begin with Genesis 1:1: "In the beginning, God. . . ." Thus, if the unbeliever is consistent with his own presupposition, he cannot logically come to faith in the God of the Bible. Thus, he must have his thinking transformed by grace. The natural man does not accept the things of the Spirit (I Cor. 2:14).

Can Christians and non-Christians cooperate successfully in certain areas?

Yes. They can cooperate because God restrains the covenant-breaker from thinking and acting consistently with his own God-defying presuppositions. But the Christian must take care to see that this cooperation with covenant-breakers is conducted on God's terms, not the unbelievers' terms. This is why biblical law is crucial for successful dominion: it spells out the principles and specifics of all responsible action, including cooperative action with unbelievers.

Do God's gifts increase or decrease over time?

His gifts to covenant-keepers increase over time. There is progress in history—spiritual, economic, scientific, and technological. Because these special gifts increase, like loaves on the table, the quantity of crumbs for the covenant-breakers also increases over time, but only to the extent that they are not fully consistent with their own God-defying presuppositions.

Will the cultural mandate (dominion covenant) of Genesis 1:28 be fulfilled?

There will not be perfect fulfillment in time and on earth, for there will always be sin prior to the final judgment. Nevertheless, there will be progressive fulfillment over time, as men more and more conform themselves to Christ's perfect humanity by means of His law, as empowered by the Holy Spirit. God's plan for the ages does not include visible, external, historical defeat for His church at the hands of Satan's forces. The death and resurrection of Christ guaranteed the visible, external, historical victory of the kingdom of God. Christ will deal with His enemies as if they were footstools, in time and on earth. "Then cometh the end, when he shall have delivered up the kingdom to God, even the Father; when he shall have put down all rule and all authority and power. For he must reign till he hath put all enemies under his feet. The last enemy that shall be destroyed is death" (I Cor. 15:24-26).

We come at last to the two questions that I left unanswered in the Preface.

"How can a world full of reprobates be considered a manifestation of the kingdom of God on earth?"

"How can unbelievers possess so much power after generations of Christian dominion?"

First, let me deal with the problem of the vast number of reprobates at the last day. We are not sure from the text of Revelation 20 that they outnumber the Christians. A well-organized army does not have to outnumber their opponents if the opponents are not ready for a war. We can be sure that Satan's forces will be sufficiently well organized to constitute a major threat to the church. It is the final gasp of the power religion. The concentration of satanic power for considerable periods of time is a possibility.

Nevertheless, we have seen these previous satanic kingdoms arise primarily during periods of declining faith in God. Why, in the midst of a faithful church, will this horde be unleashed at that final day? The answer is easy: *to end history*. It will be the last power play of God's enemies. They will rebel in the face of good moral examples. This will not be a prelude to the historic judgment of Christians, as satanic outbreaks have been in the past. It will be a prelude to the final judgment of Satan.

Satan's final rebellion is analogous to Hitler's decision to counter-attack against British and American forces in the winter of 1944, when Germany was clearly beaten. The Battle of the Bulge was briefly a fearful slaughter. This is Satan's way: suicide. All those who hate God love death.

Where will that growing army of reprobates be hiding until that final day? In churches, probably. They will remain outwardly faithful in terms of the externals of the covenant. This will increase their external blessings, their control over resources, and above all, their envy.

Second, how will they be able to accumulate so much power? We have already seen the answer: from the external blessings of God on them during the era of that final generation. Common grace will be at its maximum, as it was in Methuselah's day just before the flood. They will not be living consistently with their own philosophy of chaos. They will be forced to admit who God is, what His law is, and how the covenantal world really works. This will not lead to their regeneration; it will lead to their suicidal rebellion.

Their rebellion will grow from the inside out. This is the meaning of the release of Satan. There will be a sudden outworking of the internal covenantal rebellion of untold numbers of previously upright citizens—externally upright.

So here we have it: an answer to that troubling question for postmillennialists, "How does the postmillennialist explain the final rebellion of Satan at the end of history?" My response: "Through a biblical understanding of common grace, eschatology, and biblical law."

Postscript

By now, I have alienated every known Christian group. I have alienated the remaining Christian Reformed Church members who are orthodox by siding with the Protestant Reformed Church against Point 1 of the 1924 Synod. There is no favor in God's common grace. I have alienated the Protestant Reformed Church by arguing for postmillennialism. I have alienated the premillennialists by arguing that the separation between wheat and tares must come at the end of history, not a thousand years before the end (or, in the dispensational, pretribulational, premillennial framework, 1007 years before). I have alienated postmillennial pietists who read and delight in the works of Jonathan Edwards by arguing that Edwards' tradition was destructive to biblical law in 1740 and still is. It leads nowhere unless it matures and adopts the concept of biblical law as a tool of victory. I have alienated the Bible Presbyterian Church, since its leaders deny the dominion covenant. I have alienated Greg Bahnsen by implying that one of his published arguments isn't consistent, and even worse, that one of Meredith Kline's anti-Bahnsen arguments is. Have I missed anyone? Oh, yes, I have alienated postmillennial Arminians ("positive confession" charismatics) by arguing that the rebels in the last day are not simply backslidden Christians.

Having accomplished this, I hope that others will follow through on the outline I have sketched relating common grace, eschatology, and biblical law. Let those few who take this book seriously avoid the theological land mines that still clutter up the landscape. There are refinements that must be made, implications that must be discovered and then worked out. I hope that my contribution will make other men's tasks that much easier.

Appendix

WARFIELD'S VISION OF
VICTORY: LOST AND FOUND

*Dr. Warfield's funeral took place yesterday after-
noon at the First Church of Princeton. . . . It seemed
to me that the old Princeton—a great institution it was
—died when Dr. Warfield was carried out.*

*I am thankful for one last conversation I had with
Dr. Warfield some weeks ago. He was quite himself
that afternoon. And somehow I cannot believe that the
faith which he represented will ever really die. In the
course of the conversation I expressed my hope that to
end the present intolerable condition there might be a
great split in the Church, in order to separate the Christians from the anti-Christian propagandists. "No," he
said, "you can't split rotten wood." His expectation
seemed to be that the organized Church, dominated by
naturalism, would become so cold and dead, that people would come to see that spiritual life could be found
only outside of it, and that thus there might be a new
beginning.*

Nearly everything that I have done I have done

*with the inspiring hope that Dr. Warfield would think
well of it.*

> J. Gresham Machen
> letter to his mother
> (Feb. 19, 1921)[1]

No man can excel at everything in life. Benjamin
B. Warfield had his limitations. He understood them
and lived in terms of them. He was not a famous
preacher, nor was he a skilled bureaucrat inside the
theologically declining Northern Presbyterian
Church. Unlike Machen, a bachelor, Warfield was
not a popular instructor who mixed readily with the
students. In later years, he had the heavy burden of
caring for his invalid wife, and had little time for
church politics and social activities. His contribution
to God's church was limited and highly focused: he
wrote. He wrote volumes: scholarly books and reviews, as well as easily read essays. He was dedicated to the idea that scholarship is basic to the establishment of God's kingdom, in time and on earth,
and he was determined to do his part to bring in that
kingdom through self-disciplined, dedicated scholarship. He sat in his study, decade after decade, and
left a unique, almost unparalleled legacy of theological scholarship.

It is clear from Machen's letter to his mother that
Warfield's influence was very great on the young
scholar. If any Reformed theologian of the 1920's and

---

1. Cited in Ned B. Stonehouse, *J. Gresham Machen: A Biograph-
ical Memoir* (Grand Rapids, Michigan: Eerdmans, 1954), p. 310.

1930's deserves to be recognized as Warfield's spiritual-intellectual heir, it is J. Gresham [GRESSum] Machen [MAYchen].

Machen's Battle

Machen went beyond Warfield in many ways. He was independently wealthy, so he did not have to worry about where his next meal was coming from, even if he was fired from, or resigned from, his teaching post at Princeton Theological Seminary. His relationships with his students substituted for the wife and children he never had. His students responded with both affection and dedication, and this was to enable Machen to lead an institutional challenge in the Presbyterian Church, U.S.A. Machen was a scrapper, perhaps not by temperament, but by timing, choice, and abilities. In this sense, he was not an heir of Warfield's personality, but he was an heir to Warfield's theological vision. He applied Warfield's theology to historical circumstances.

Warfield had not been the man to launch a defensive battle against all of modernism, or even modernism within the Presbyterian Church. The timing was wrong. The conservative members of the Church in Warfield's era had virtually no awareness concerning the impending theological crisis. After the famous and successful Briggs heresy trial in 1893, the Presbyterian Church did not again attempt to remove a major theological leader for reasons of heresy. The liberals understood this weakness on the part of conservatives—an unwillingness continually to "cleanse the temple" theologically. By the end of his long career, in 1920, Warfield knew how such a defensive fight would turn out.

Machen's challenge to the modernists was front-page news in the *New York Times*, from 1923 until he and his faithful little band of 34 mostly younger pastors—what the Church calls "teaching elders"— 17 ruling elders, and 79 laymen left the Church in June of 1936. Today, we find it difficult to believe that theology was a major issue in the secular press, but it was, insofar as theological issues determined who would control the funds, boards, and influence of the denominations in the inter-war decades.

Warfield's name had not been featured in the newspapers of his day, for he was content to remain at his calling. He rallied no troops, issued no manifestos, and appealed no judicial decisions through the Presbyterian court system. What he did was to lay down an intellectual and theological foundation that might be used in the future, he believed, to reconstruct the entire ecclesiastical order, and after that, the world.

"Old Princeton"

It is generally acknowledged that Princeton Theological Seminary was, from its founding in the early nineteenth century until Machen's departure in 1929, the world's leading academic institution of conservative Protestant scholarship. It was almost a family enterprise, so dominant were the names of Hodge and Alexander in the nineteenth century. Benjamin B. Warfield was the last of these giants whose name is exclusively associated with Princeton.

The Princeton theological tradition has been
studied by several scholars. It was noted for its strict
adherence to the inerrancy of Scripture and its proc-
lamation of Calvinist theology. It was a dedicated
creedal institution. Its adherence to the Westminster
Confession of Faith placed it at the forefront of Reformed Presbyterianism throughout the nineteenth
century. It maintained high standards of scholarship. While Princeton University in the late nineteenth century began to drift theologically under the
rule of President McCosh, who adopted certain
principles of evolutionism in an attempt to fuse
Christianity and modern thought, Princeton Seminary under the Hodges did not waver. Charles Hodge
recognized the enormous threat to orthodoxy which
Darwinism posed, and he rejected it vigorously.[2]

Darwinism's Threat

By the turn of the century, however, the inroads
of Darwinism in conservative Christian intellectual
circles had begun to take its toll. The Seminary's
faculty members were not willing to go into print
with anti-evolutionary articles, let alone whole
books. As American seminary education became
ever-more narrow, confined to biblical languages
(which the colleges no longer taught extensively),
preaching, and theology proper, concern over the
confrontation between "science and Scripture" fell
into the background. Christian scholars of that era

---

2. Charles Hodge, *Systematic Theology*, 3 vols. (Grand Rapids,
Michigan: Eerdmans, [1871] 1959), II, pp. 12-24.

had no body of scientific creationist scholarship to rely upon as a first line defense against Darwinism. (There were numerous conflicting varieties of Darwinism, it should be understood. The modern Darwinian synthesis—which has begun to disintegrate since the early 1970's—had not yet gained universal acceptance. The confrontation between Christianity and Darwinism was not yet visibly total, as it became after World War I.) Christians did not yet understand just how all encompassing Darwinism is as a philosophy. They did not fully recognize how the tenets of evolution create a rival worldview in every academic discipline and in every area of life—not just in biology and historical geology, but in politics, economics, law, psychology, and philosophy.

Warfield did not insist on a six-day creation. Indeed, he announced in a *Princeton Theological Review* essay (1911) that "The question of the antiquity of man has itself no theological significance. It is to theology, as such, a matter of entire indifference how long man has existed on earth. . . . The Bible does not assign a brief span to human history; this is done only by a particular mode of interpreting the Biblical data, which is found on examination to rest on no solid basis."[3]

Warfield, in one brief essay, gave away the case for biblical creationism, and thereby undercut the Christian's defense of that most fundamental of doctrines (according to Van Til), the Creator-creature

---

3. "On the Antiquity and the Unity of the Human Race," in *Biblical and Theological Studies* (Philadelphia: Presbyterian & Reformed, 1952), pp. 238-39.

distinction. The blurring (and outright denial) of this distinction is the essence of all pagan religions, and especially of Darwinism, the religion of modern man. Warfield, heavily influenced by the humanism he sought to refute, reflected the softening of the "old Princeton."

Seminary Education: The "Soft Underbelly"

Because of the high emphasis Presbyterians have always put on a highly educated priesthood, to the point of distinguishing "teaching elders" (seminary graduates) from "ruling elders" (laymen elected to office), the Church was innately vulnerable to long-term infiltration. The "ruling elders"—laymen— were generally more interested in peace, evangelism, Church growth, and therefore ecclesiastical unity. The "teaching elders," who might have been expected to uphold Presbyterianism's rigorous doctrinal standards, were graduates of seminaries, and seminaries were innately compromised: they recognized higher academic degrees as the main criterion of permanent ecclesiastical positions, but the humanist world which granted such degrees was hostile to the orthodox faith. Thus, the lure of Harvard, Princeton (University), Yale, and the German theological cesspools was too great, just as it has been too great for Christian colleges in our day. Simultaneously, the "good old boy" mentality of the "teaching elders" eroded the willingness of their fellow graduates to boot out heretics. Old friends from seminary, after all, had to be recognized as fellow "runners of the academic gauntlet." Besides, their former professors had graduated them. This was not quite the same as having baptized their theological views, but over time, this is what graduation from seminary came to mean. The seminary degree was, after 1893 (and probably from 1812 onward), very nearly a guarantee of eventual ecclesiastical licensure.

Warfield recognized the threat, but he only discussed it publicly late in his career. He saw the seminary as a *support institution*, one with distinct limitations. "It is not the function of the seminary to give young men their entire training for the ministry. That is the concern of the presbytery; and no other organization can supersede the presbytery in this business. The seminary is only an instrument which the presbytery uses in training young men for the ministry. *An* instrument, not *the* instrument. The presbytery uses other instruments also in this work."[4] But no matter how hard he or other Calvinistic Presbyterians might proclaim the legitimate sovereignty of the presbytery, their rationalism and their respect for the institutions of higher (humanist) learning eventually undercut their warnings.

The implicit rationalism of the old Presbyterianism led into the quicksand of certification. Once a man had earned his degree from an approved seminary, it became very difficult for laymen to challenge him when he sought ordination, and the very fact that he had a degree made him very nearly an "initi-

---

4. "The Purpose of the Seminary," *The Presbyterian* (Nov. 22, 1917); reprinted in *Selected Shorter Writings of Benjamin B. Warfield— I*, edited by John E. Meeter (Nutley, New Jersey: Presbyterian & Reformed, 1970), p. 374.

ate in advance" among the "teaching elders," who distinguished themselves institutionally (and, I would guess, psychologically) from "ruling elders" by their possession of an earned degree. Who, then, within the conservative camp was ready for a fight with degree-holding heretics within the camp? Hardly anyone after 1893.

"Old Princeton's" Weakness: Apologetics

The liberals had a difficult time in their capture of the Northern Presbyterians because of the rigorous orthodoxy of the Westminster standards. It took them half a century. But Princeton and McCormick Seminaries could not withstand indefinitely the pressure of humanist education. It was not merely a question of the lack of numbers of Old School advocates. It was a much deeper problem than Church politics. Old School Presbyterianism was itself rationalistic in its apologetic methodology—its philosophical defense of the faith. Its apologetic method was based on the belief in the existence of "shared first principles of logic" between the saved and the lost. This was essentially a form of *epistemological "inclusivism."* Warfield wrote: "All minds are of the same essential structure. . . ."[5] Because they have the same mental structure, unbelievers are subject to arguments for Christianity that appeal to a common human reason. It was this aspect of the apologetics

---

5. Warfield, "Introduction to Francis R. Beattie's *Apologetics*" (1903); reprinted in John E. Meeter (ed.), *Selected Shorter Writings of Benjamin B. Warfield—II* (Nutley, New Jersey: Presbyterian & Reformed, 1973), p. 103.

of Princeton Seminary that Westminster Seminary philosopher-theologian Cornelius Van Til criticized for half a century as Princeton's weak link theologically.[6]

Warfield was a postmillennialist. He believed that the gospel of Christ will triumph on earth before Christ returns again in judgment. But what undermined Warfield's eschatology was his reliance on human reason — the "Old Princeton" rationalist apologetic method — as an important basis of this great revival. It is difficult for us to believe that anyone in the post-Darwin, or even post-Kant world could have believed in reason as *the* means of evangelism, but Warfield did. No more vigorous defense of "the primacy of the intellect" as the Christian's tool of dominion can be found in Christian literature.

> The part that Apologetics has to play in the Christianizing of the world is rather a primary part, and it is a conquering part. It is the distinction of Christianity that it has come into the world clothed with the mission to *reason* its way to its dominion. Other religions may appeal to the sword, or seek some other way to propagate themselves. Christianity makes its appeal to

---

6. His criticisms of Charles Hodge's *Systematic Theology* appear under the heading "Less Consistent Calvinism," in his classroom syllabus, *Apologetics* (Westminster Theological Seminary, 1959), pp. 47ff. His criticisms of B. B. Warfield are found in his book, *A Christian Theory of Knowledge* (Nutley, New Jersey: Presbyterian & Reformed, 1969), pp. 229f. Van Til was a graduate of Princeton University (Ph.D. under A. A. Bowman) and Princeton Theological Seminary (Th.M.), and he taught at Princeton Seminary for one year prior to the division in 1929.

right reason, and stands out among all religions, therefore, as distinctively "the Apologetic
religion." It is solely by reasoning that it has
come thus far on its way to its kingship. And it
is solely by reasoning that it will put all its enemies under its feet.[7]

The *credentials* of Christianity, said Warfield, are
its *logic*. "It stands calmly over against the world with
its credentials in its hands, and fears no contentions
of men."[8] But these credentials were collapsing in
Warfield's day, and did collapse in Machen's day — in
the face of Darwinism, post-Heisenberg science, and
the rise of secular humanism. Warfield believed in
the triumph of Christianity through logic, but it was
as a result of the *continual intellectual defeats* suffered by
Christians who used the rationalism of "Protestant
scholasticism," which Warfield taught, that conservative churches went into a fifty-year eclipse after
1925. The "logic" which Warfield proclaimed turned
out to be a "drawbridge" by which humanists crossed
Christianity's defensive moat and began to batter
down its gates. Warfield's much-praised "credentials"
turned out to be first and foremost *humanism's* credentials, both in principle (common-ground logic)
and institutionally (seminary and university
degrees).

This weakness of Princeton's apologetic methodology had been present from the very beginning. In

---

7. Warfield, *Shorter Writings — II*, pp. 99-100.
8. *Ibid.*, p. 100.

an informative introduction to the writings of several of the great Princeton theologians, Mark Noll offers a fine summary of the presuppositions—common-ground reasoning—of what has come to be called the Scottish common-sense philosophy. It was this apologetic approach which Van Til, using a consistently "presuppositionalist" apologetics in the tradition of Dutchmen Abraham Kuyper and Herman Bavinck, challenged from the earliest stages of his career. Noll writes:

> This approach laid great stress on the "common sense" of humankind. It argued that normal people, using responsibly the information provided by their senses, actually grasped thereby the real world. Furthermore, an exercise of the "moral sense," a faculty analogous in all important ways to physical senses, gave humans immediate knowledge about the nature of their own minds. And because all humans, humanity in *common*, were able to grasp the truth of the world in this way—in fact, could not live unless they took for granted that truth was available in this way—this *common sense* could provide the basis for a full-scale philosophy as well. . . . The Scottish philosophers regarded truth as a static entity, open equally to all people wherever they lived, in the present or past. They placed a high premium on scientific investigation. They were deeply committed to an empirical method that made much of gathering relevant facts into logical

wholes. They abhorred "speculation" and "metaphysics" as unconscionable flights from the basic realities of the physical world and the human mind. And at least some of them assumed that this approach could be used to convince all rational souls of the truth of Christianity, the necessity of traditional social order, and the capacity of scientific methods to reveal whatever may be learned about the world.[9]

It should not be surprising to find that Machen, as the last of the "Old Princetonians," spoke of the need of defending a "scientific theology."[10] His debt to the "old Princeton," including its experientialism, was very great.[11] The humanists of the twentieth century have successfully called in all such debts to nineteenth-century rationalism. The debtors went epistemologically bankrupt.

Van Til's approach takes the best of both Kuyper and Warfield. In contrast to Kuyper, Van Til argues that we can do more than preach to the natural (unregenerate) man. We can show him, by the premises of his own philosophy, that he has no place to stand

9. Mark Noll, "Introduction," in Noll (ed.), *The Princeton Theology, 1812-1921* (Grand Rapids, Michigan: Baker, 1983), p. 31.
10. Machen, *Christianity and Liberalism* (New York: Macmillan, 1923), p. 17.
11. On Machen's promotion of the idea of the importance of an experience from God, see *ibid.*, p. 67. On the "old Princeton" and its theology of experience, see W. Andrew Hoffecker, *Piety and the Princeton Theologians* (Phillipsburg, New Jersey: Presbyterian & Reformed, 1981).

epistemologically. Van Til uses the "transcendental" proof of God: that without *presupposing the God of the Bible,* man can say *nothing* logical. In contrast to Warfield, Van Til argues that all unregenerate men use their anti-God presuppositions to come to the "logical" conclusion that the God of the Bible cannot possibly exist. Therefore, if we allow the natural man to use his logic in this way — if we allow him to assume that we all begin with the same presuppositions about reality as autonomous men — then we cannot deal with him effectively. We have violated the Bible's first principle, namely, that it is God who is sovereign, and therefore man has no autonomy.

Warfield wanted to appeal to the common "right reason" of man in his defense of the faith, but, as Van Til comments, "in Apologetics, Warfield wanted to operate in neutral territory with the non-believer. He thought that this was the only way to show to the unbeliever that theism and Christianity are objectively true. He sought for an objectivity that bridged the gulf between Kuyper's 'natural' and special principles." Then, he makes himself clear: "I have chosen the position of Abraham Kuyper."[12]

We must confront the natural man with the bankruptcy of his position. We do need to challenge him logically, but only by using God's logic, because "no challenge is presented to him unless it is shown him that on his *principle* he would destroy all truth and meaning. Then, if the Holy Spirit enlightens

---

12. Cornelius Van Til, *The Defense of the Faith* (2nd ed.; Philadelphia: Presbyterian & Reformed, 1963), p. 265.

him spiritually, he will be born again 'unto knowledge' and adopt with love the principle he was previously anxious to destroy."[13]

Van Til self-consciously attempts to build on the work of both the Princetonians and the Dutch. There is a common ground only in the sense of God in every man, the image of God. Man knows enough to condemn himself before God. We are to do more than preach to the lost, says Van Til. And we must do more than argue with the lost in terms of their presupposition of autonomy. He concludes *The Defense of the Faith* with these words: "Standing on the shoulders of Warfield and Kuyper we honor them best if we build on the main thrust of their thought rather than if we insist on carrying on what is inconsistent with their basic position. Then we are most faithful to Calvin and St. Paul."[14]

The two "nations" within the Northern Presbyterian Church were unquestionably divided theologically: humanism vs. Christianity. They were not equally divided methodologically. Princeton's common ground apologetics softened the radical intellectual distinction between the saved and the lost because rationalist apologetics failed to see that the incompatible *ethical* presuppositions—saved vs. lost—created inescapable differences in men's interpretation of the facts and their use of logic.

Princeton's error in apologetics led to an overesti-

---

13. *Ibid.*, p. 266.
14. *Ibid.*, p. 299.

268 DOMINION AND COMMON GRACE

mation of the role of the intellect in challenging men to believe in Christ. This, in turn, led to an overestimation of the skills imparted by higher education. Higher education, then as now, was a Trojan Horse —a gift of the "Greeks" which the Princetonians should have mistrusted. This faith in higher education, meaning education constructed in terms of the principle of the autonomy of human reason (yes, even "right reason"), served in effect as a bridge across the great divide over which theological liberals could pass. The "passport" which got the humanists across the bridge was the *earned academic degree*. It could be argued that it was a similar overestimation of the benefits of classical education which helped to undermine the Puritans in the seventeenth century and the Calvinists who followed Jonathan Edwards in the eighteenth.

"Old Princeton's" Strength: Eschatology

There is no question about the dominant eschatological heritage of nineteenth-century American Presbyterianism in general, and Princeton Seminary in particular. It was postmillennial. There was no more eloquent spokesman of this postmillennialism than B. B. Warfield. His optimism was unbounded concerning the future of Christ's gospel on earth prior to Christ's second coming at the final judgment. The kingdom of Satan will be rolled back. The earth will be filled with the saved and their works.

It is significant that Warfield's opponent in this debate over the extent of the saved on earth was the

Dutch theologian, Abraham Kuyper, just as Bavinck and Kuyper were his chosen opponents in the debate over apologetic methodology. Warfield rejected the Dutchmen's amillennial eschatology, just as he rejected their presuppositional apologetics. In fact, Warfield begins his discussion of the question "are there few that be saved?" (the title of his essay) by challenging Kuyper's statement that "The idea of some Christians that the whole of Europe is sometime to be Christianized, and after a while the entirety of the human race is to bow the knee to Jesus, cannot be maintained. The Holy Scriptures contradict this erroneous idea: Mat. 20:16, 'For many are called, but few chosen,' Mat. 7:14; Lk. 13:23."

This is not the place to offer a detailed summary of Warfield's detailed rejoinder to Kuyper. The essay can be found in *Biblical and Theological Studies*. The important point here is that there were two fundamental theological debates within the world of Calvinism in Warfield's day, primarily between the American Presbyterians and the Dutch. The disputed issues were apologetics and eschatology. That debate was taken up by Warfield, and, as it turned out, he was the last important American Presbyterian scholar to focus on these two issues until R. J. Rushdoony reintroduced both issues in the 1960's and 1970's. Rushdoony answered both Warfield and Kuyper by adopting the postmillennial optimism of the "Old Princeton," and by rejecting the "Old Princeton's" apologetics in favor of Van Til's final version of the older Kuyper-Bavinck position. That theological fusion launched what is now known as the Christian Reconstruction movement. (Two other important issues also make up "Reconstructionism": biblical law and predestination, although the latter doctrine is not held by many Baptists and Pentecostals who have been influenced by the "Reconstructionists." Rushdoony was the first theologian to adhere to all four positions and to develop a consistent worldview in terms of all four.)

Warfield's vision concerning the world-conquering nature of the gospel helps us to understand his unwillingness to encourage a young Machen in his proposed battle to toss out the growing legion of modernists and liberals in the Northern Presbyterian Church. Warfield was a Presbyterian; no one could doubt that. But Warfield's vision extended beyond the denomination in which he had worked all of his life. The failures of any one denomination in one time period and in one geographical region did not overwhelm his long-term optimism. Yes, his Church was close to defecting from the orthodox faith. Indeed, its inability to enforce the Westminster standards, and the General Assembly's substitution in 1910 of five watered-down "fundamentalist" doctrines as the test of orthodoxy, indicated that the Church had long since given up the historic Presbyterian standards. But this did not overly concern Warfield. Christianity is broader than the Northern Presbyterian Church and of greater duration. The battle is long-term. Warfield's eschatological vision could not be undermined by short-term setbacks. Rotten wood, after all, is rotten. It is fit only for burning.

Westminster Seminary: 1929-1964

Westminster Seminary has always claimed to be the heir of the "Old Princeton." In terms of its commitment to the Westminster Confession of Faith and to Princeton's high standards of scholarship, this claim was true, at least until the mid-1960's, when the Administration began to make a systematic effort to broaden the Seminary's financial and recruiting base, and to become a less visibly Calvinistic and more "evangelical" institution. This shift occurred when Edmund P. Clowney was finally made president of the Seminary, rather than simply acting president. It also coincided with the intellectual, institutional, and religious disruptions of the 1965-70 period, which engulfed the whole Western world. From that point onward, Westminster's claim to be the "Old Princeton" became questionable. There is no heir to the "Old Princeton" any longer.

In two important aspects, however, Westminster's claim to be the heir of "Old Princeton" was always a myth. Westminster hired Cornelius Van Til to teach apologetics in 1930, and Van Til was a Dutchman—indeed, as he likes to say of himself, a stubborn Dutchman. He was a follower of Kuyper and Bavinck in both his apologetic methodology and his eschatology. He was a presuppositionalist and an amillennialist. On these two crucial issues, he was non-Princeton.

This is not to say that Van Til's apologetic method was adhered to (or even understood) by his faculty colleagues. Only Edward J. Young, among the prominent faculty members, ever seemed to adopt Van Til's principle of circular reasoning, and this was as a result of Young's reading Rushdoony's book, *By What Standard?* (1959), rather than reading Van Til. I studied briefly under both Van Til and systematic theologian John Murray. I doubt that Murray ever relied on Van Til's apologetics to any degree, and Murray's adoption of a mild postmillennialism late in his career (with his studies of Romans 11) was at odds with Van Til's eschatology. What I am arguing here is that the older Princeton apologetics that Machen held to was no longer taught formally at Westminster, nor was the older postmillennialism that Machen also believed.

Yet even in Machen's career, the importance of eschatology was muted. The older theological commitment had begun to fade. Machen never emphasized eschatology in his writings. When I asked Westminster's long-time church historian Paul Woolley in 1964 what eschatology Machen held, he replied: "To the extent that he ever mentioned it, Machen was a postmillennialist." There is no question that he was opposed to premillennialism, and not just dispensational premillennialism, for he said so clearly in *Christianity and Liberalism* (p. 49). But there is no sign in any of his writings that he relied heavily on postmillennialism as a motivating concept in his battle against the modernists.

When Machen pulled out of Princeton in the summer of 1929, he had few followers from Princeton's faculty. Only four men were to forsake Princeton's security for the uncertain venture at Westminster: Robert Dick Wilson, who was Professor of Old Testament (and who died a year later); John Murray, who had not been a full faculty member at Princeton, came a year later; Cornelius Van Til, who had taught at Princeton for one year, left Princeton for the pastorate for one more year before joining Machen, and Oswald T. Allis, an Old Testament specialist who was postmillennial but who never wrote on the topic openly as a postmillennialist, even in his book on eschatology which refutes dispensationalism: *Prophecy and the Church*. Three recent graduates of Princeton also joined: Allan A. MacRae (Old Testament), a premillennialist; Paul Woolley (church history), a premillennialist; and Ned B. Stonehouse (New Testament), an amillennialist of Dutch origins, whose family name had been Steenhuizen, and who belonged to the Christian Reformed Church. Later additions to the faculty included Edward J. Young (Old Testament), an amillennialist, and R. B. Kuiper (practical theology), an amillennialist from the Christian Reformed Church; and John H. Skilton (New Testament), who was amillennial.

Thus, from 1930 on, there were only two postmillennialists on the faculty: Machen and Allis. Allis resigned at the end of the term in 1936 in order to protest Machen's requirement that Westminster faculty members proclaim their support of his Independent Board for Presbyterian Foreign Missions. Machen died on January 1, 1937, two months after Carl McIntyre and the premillennialists had kicked him out as president of the Independent Board. That left no postmillennialists on the faculty. From that time until Norman Shepherd joined the faculty in 1963, there were no postmillennialists teaching full time at Westminster, and Shepherd's eschatological views did not come out clearly in his lectures. Worse; in his class on New Testament biblical theology, he assigned the amillennial textbook, *The Pauline Eschatology* by Geerhardus Vos (1862-1949). (Fortunately for postmillennialists, Vos had one of the worst writing styles imaginable, and it is almost as difficult to remember any of his arguments as it is to remember the arguments of Meredith G. Kline on biblical symbolism. It was a sign of the preliminary Dutch influence in the "Old Princeton" that Princeton had Vos teaching biblical theology from 1893, the year of the Briggs trial, until his retirement in 1932. As a result, biblical theology within Calvinistic circles has been generally assumed to be the invention and exclusive monopoly of amillennialists. That day has ended, as the writings of James Jordan and David Chilton indicate—and they, unlike Vos and Kline, are readable.)

John Murray had studied theology under Vos at Princeton, and Vos's influence in his thinking was strong. As a systematic theologian, Murray always had great respect for the discipline of biblical theology—the idea of progressive revelation and progressive clarity, from Genesis to Revelation. This was Vos's influence. Van Til related after Murray's death that Murray had advised him not to accept the chair of systematic theology at Calvin seminary after Prof. Berkhof's death, because, "To teach systematics properly one must, first of all, be a biblical exegete. After that, one must be a biblical theologian in the way that Professor Geerhardus Vos had been a biblical theologian in his day."[15] Murray wrote that "Biblical theology is indispensable to systematic theology."[16] He also held Vos's amillennial viewpoint until late in his own teaching career. He became a mild postmillennialist in the late 1950's, partially as a result of his discussions in Canada with Roderick Campbell, and unquestionably as a result of his own study of Romans 11: the conversion of the Jews. But initially he limited his public discussion of Romans 11 to the Sunday school classes he taught off campus.

His spring, 1964 lectures in his senior systematics class on eschatology were based on old and apparently unrevised notes, and were therefore still amillennial in focus, while his lectures on Romans 11, given earlier in the day, were postmillennial.[17] I attended both classes, and was astounded at the schizophrenia involved. Senior systematics was required for graduation; the Romans class was optional. As a result, there was an undercurrent of confusion among the student body as to exactly what Murray was teaching. Eschatologically speaking, there were two John Murrays in the mid-1960's, but as far as the majority of his students ever knew, there was only one: the amillennialist. (His lectures on Romans 11, and my own reading of Revelation 12, brought me from ultradispensationalism to postmillennialism in the spring of 1964.)

---

15. Cited by Iain Murray, "Life of John Murray," in *The Collected Writings of John Murray*, 4 vols. (Edinburgh: Banner of Truth Trust, 1982), III, p. 94.

16. John Murray, "Systematic Theology," *ibid.*, IV, p. 16.

17. John Murray, *The Epistle to the Romans*, 2 vols. (Grand Rapids, Michigan: Eerdmans, 1965), vol. 2.

In short, from the beginning, there had been a "Dutch Invasion" of Westminster Seminary. The intellectual leadership of a seminary is usually found in three departments: systematic theology, New Testament studies, and apologetics. All three departments were dominated by amillennialists from the beginning at Westminster, and still are. Thus, with the demise of Princeton Seminary after the departure of Machen, and the overwhelming intellectual and *financial* support of Westminster coming from Christian Reformed (Dutch) circles from the beginning, a theological vacuum appeared in orthodox American Presbyterianism. The postmillennial vision of the older Presbyterianism faded, and faded rapidly. Only one man's name was associated with Calvinistic postmillennialism from the 1940's through the early 1960's: Loraine Boettner. But Boettner had remained in the old Presbyterian Church, so his influence was nil in the breakaway churches. (Canadian Roderick Campbell's *Israel and the New Covenant*, published in 1954, did not sell well, and went out of print in the mid-1960's. It was not reprinted until 1981, and the money was put up by the Geneva Divinity School Press, a "Reconstructionist" organization.)

The Recovery of Warfield's Vision

Alva J. McClain, a leader in the dispensationalist camp, announced in 1956 that "Devout Postmillennialism has virtually disappeared."[18] Hal Lindsey

---

18. "Postmillennialism as a Philosophy of History," in W. Culbertson and H. B. Centz (eds.), *Understanding the Times* (Grand Rapids, Michigan: Zondervan, 1956), p. 22.

was even more outspoken (with less justification) than McClain, for he wrote 14 years later: "No self-respecting scholar who looks at the world conditions and at the accelerating decline of Christian influence today is a 'postmillenialist.'"[19] The great irony here was that much of the declining influence of Christianity, 1870-1970, was the product of dispensational theology's implied doctrinal justification of cultural impotence and retreat. For a century, dispensationalism and amillennialism combined to remove the hope of earthly success from Christians. Then, having castrated the sheep, they explained the unfruitfulness of the sheep on God's timetable. God supposedly has decided not to bring to earth in history a visible manifestation of His kingdom prior to Jesus' second coming. Therefore, cultural unfruitfulness is to become the Christian way of life. God has called us to earthly defeat. We were born to lose.

Postmillennialism was not dead, as they supposed; it was only hibernating. Like a newly awakened (and hungry) grizzly, the postmillennialist movement has come out of its long winter sleep. This time, however, it is armed more securely than it was in Warfield's day. It has a vision of victory, which was Warfield's vision. It also has a tool of dominion, biblical law, as well as a new self-confidence based on a better understanding of human reason: presuppositional apologetics. The presuppositional apologetic methodology of Van Til is what Rushdoony set forth

---

19. Lindsey, *The Late, Great Planet Earth* (Grand Rapids, Michigan: Zondervan, 1970), p. 176.

as the epistemological foundation of "Reconstructionism" in *By What Standard?* (1959), a decade before
the term "Christian Reconstruction" was invented.

The rapid spread of "Reconstructionist" ideas
through the Christian community can be explained
by many factors, but perhaps the most important
ones are these:

1. The rise of the six-day creationist movement
after 1960. (Rushdoony helped launch this by getting
Presbyterian & Reformed to publish Morris & Whit-
comb's *Genesis Flood*, after other Christian publishers
had turned it down.) This has helped to overcome
the belief that Christians just have to make an intellectual deal with evolutionism. This deal-seeking
had paralyzed Christian scholarship since 1925.

2. The visible disintegration of humanism after
1963. The enemy is no longer self-confident in the
universal logic of neutral reason. Everything is now
up for grabs, and everyone is grabbing. With their
loss of faith in universal neutral reason, humanists
are less secure about challenging the validity of a
consistent Christian world view.

3. The *Roe v. Wade* decision in 1973, which struck
down state laws against abortion. The literal life-
and-death issue of abortion reveals the truth of Van
Til's apologetic principle: *there can be no neutrality.*
Either the unborn infant lives or is destroyed. There
is no in-between. The fundamentalists are now
mobilizing, as they have not done since Prohibition.
The sin of abortion is being challenged in the name
of an explicitly biblical and Old Testament law system. This has been the first practical (tactical) step in

the reintroduction of Christians' faith in biblical law.

4. The rise of the independent Christian school movement since 1965. To pull children out of the humanist public schools is now seen as a religious duty by millions of parents. New curricula are now needed. Thus, there has been a quest for "reconstructed" textbooks—books that are different from state textbooks. The battle for the mind has at last become a visible reality to Christians who previously had believed in intellectual neutrality.

5. The rise of television's mass-appeal "electronic ministries." It is difficult to mobilize support (read: increase donations) by means of a theology of defeat. Supporters will not give enthusiastically to "just another ministry of failure"; they can give to local churches if they are moved by an eschatology of failure. After all, it is the "Rapture" guarantee of the local church which had brought so many people in, 1925-1975. To compete, the T.V. ministries had to offer something new. Many offer the grim story of humanist tyranny; the audience gets angry and wants to fight. Why fight to lose? Thus, the language of avowed premillennialists has become postmillennial. This has "softened the market" for a revival of Warfield's vision of victory.

Conclusion

We are now witnessing the beginning of a true *paradigm shift*, as Thomas Kuhn has called it. The Christian community in the United States has at last begun to adopt the intellectual foundations of a new worldview, and this is always the first step in the replacement of a dying civilization which is based on a dying worldview. It happened in Rome. It happened to the medieval world. It happened in the last century to orthodoxy. It is now happening simultaneously to secular humanism, and its religious accomplice, Christian pietism. Warfield would be pleased. The day of victory draws nigh. The rotten wood is ready for burning, and a new civilization is being prepared to replace it.

SCRIPTURE INDEX

OLD TESTAMENT

NEW TESTAMENT

INDEX

Marxism &, 186, 189
power vs., 105, 114, 117, 129,
131, 174, 189
self-confidence vs., 127
victory vs., 128, 134, 239
Chilton, David, xvi
Chinese, 171, 226-27
Christian Reconstruction,
278-79
Christian Reformed Church, 6,
109-10
Christians
consistency, 132
creeds separate, 151
empowered by Spirit, 140-42
impotence?, 117-119
power religion accepted by,
238
self-consciousness, 128,
setting the agenda, 193
city on hill, 155-56, 219
Clowney, E. P., 271
coals of fire
Canaanites, 55, 207, 210
good deeds produce, 27-28,
44-45, 51-52, 93
final rebellion, 115
Noah's generation, 208
coherence, 197
Commodus, 185
common curse, 242-43
common grace
biblical law &, 94, 171
continuity, 3
cross &, 58-59
crumbs, 5-6, 92, 94
curse's prelude, 161
external consequence, 25
evil &, 210
flood, 207-9

future grace, 91, 98, 242
history, 15, 103
increases over time, 94
judgment &, 3, 165
later grace, 91-92
power &, 250
reduction of, 102
restraint of sin, 105, 129
sustaining, 241
undeveloped, 190
withdrawal of, 80-81
(see also: coals of fire)
common ground, 247, 195, 196
Communists, 130, 185-86, 191
competition, 70, 238
compound growth (see: growth)
Connecticut & revival, 174
consistency
Christians', 33, 234
covenant-breakers aren't, 33,
216, 218-19
God's restraint of, 48, 51, 105,
246
(see also: chaos, inconsistency)
continuity
common grace &, 3, 165
history, 2, 66, 74, 215, 244
two kinds of love, 205
Van Til's error, 103
(see also: discontinuity)
cooperation, 58, 247
covenant
blessing &, 25-26, 95, 145, 161
cursing &, 32
good and evil in history, 116,
191
life is, 34
love &, 205
positive feedback, 112
creeds, 101, 115, 151

labor, 58
lake of fire, 31
Latin America, 230
law
  biblical law, 94, 120, 129
  common, 25
  condemnation by, 28
  cosmonomic, 120, 135-37
  evaluation, 72
  four types, 135
  God respects, 54
  grace, 28, 49-52
  Israel, 194
  judgment standards, 52, 63
  knowledge of, 54-57
  love &, 27, 28
  Marxist, 228
  moral, 119, 120
  natural, 115, 120, 121, 152, 195
  neutral, 71
  power through, 96, 97, 129
  recovery of, 241
  restraint of sin, 49
  salvation &, 173
  tool of dominion, 46, 60, 72,
    132, 145
  tyranny of, 69
  victory &, 134
  weapon, 155
  work of, 54, 60, 63, 94, 95,
    116, 171, 219, 245
  (see also: antinomianism)
Lewis, C. S., 148-53, 190
liberation theology, 188, 229-30
lifespans, 83, 160, 169, 172, 208
Lindsey, Hal, 276-77
logic
  humanist, 204
  two kinds, 202-5
Lot, 163-64, 167

love 17, 27, 205-7

Machen, J. Gresham
  apologetics, 265
  postmillennial, 272
  scrapper, 255
  Warfield &, 253-54
Magog, ix
Mao, 238
marriage, 206
Marx, Karl 71, 183, 187, 224-26
Marxism 187-88, 227-30
Mather, Cotton 184
May Day, 223
McClain, Alva, 276
McIntyre, Carl, 273
Medo-Persia, 213
mercy, 2
Methuselah, 114, 160, 207, 250
mind, 197, 237, 239
Miranda, José, 229-30
miscarriage, 169
Moses, 212
Murray, John, 87n, 176n, 272,
  274-75
mysticism, 136, 152

natural law, 115, 195
natural man, 247
nature, 99
neutrality, 71, 116
New Heaven, 30, 31, 68, 72,
  169, 243
New Left, 187
New Mexico, 233
Newton, Isaac, 184
Noah
  coals of fire, 208
  Ham's sin, 221
  lifespans, 165, 208

Dr. Gary North
Institute for Christian Economics
P.O. Box 8000
Tyler, TX 75711

Dear Dr. North:

I read about your organization in your book, *Dominion and Common Grace*. I understand that you publish several newsletters that are sent out for six months free of charge. I would be interested in receiving them:

☐ *Biblical Economics Today*
Christian Reconstruction
and *Dominion Strategies*

Please send any other information you have concerning your program.

_____
name

_____
address

_____
city, state, zip

☐ I'm enclosing a tax-deductible donation to help defray expenses.

The *Biblical Blueprints Series* is a multi-volume book series that gives Biblical solutions for the problems facing our culture today. Each book deals with a specific topic in a simple, easy to read style such as economics, government, law, crime and punishment, welfare and poverty, taxes, money and banking, politics, the environment, retirement, and much more.

Each book can be read in one evening and will give you the basic Biblical principles on each topic. Each book concludes with three chapters on how to apply the principles in your life, the church and the nation. Every chapter is summarized so that the entire book can be absorbed in just a few minutes.

As you read these books, you will discover hundreds of new ways to serve God. Each book will show you ways that you can start to implement God's plan in your own life. As hundreds of thousands join you, and millions more begin to follow the example set, a civilization can be changed.

Why will people change their lives? Because they will see God's blessings on those who live by His Word (Deuteronomy 4:6-8).

Each title in the *Biblical Blueprints Series* is available in a deluxe paperback edition for $6.95, or a classic leatherbound edition for $14.95.

The following titles are scheduled for publication in 1986:

- Introduction to Dominion: Biblical Blueprints on Dominion
- Honest Money: Biblical Blueprints on Money and Banking
- Who Owns the Family?: Biblical Blueprints on the Family and the State
- In the Shadow of Plenty: Biblical Blueprints on Welfare and Poverty
- Liberator of the Nations: Biblical Blueprints on Political Action
- Inherit the Earth: Biblical Blueprints on Economics
- Chariots of God: Biblical Blueprints on Defense
- The Children Trap: Biblical Blueprints on Education
- Entangling Alliances: Biblical Blueprints on Foreign Policy
- Ruler of the Nations: Biblical Blueprints on Government
- Protection of the Innocent: Biblical Blueprints on Crime and Punishment

Additional Volumes of the Biblical Blueprints Series are scheduled for 1987 and 1988.

Please send more information concerning this program.

_____
name

_____
address

_____
city, state, zip

Institute for Christian Economics • P.O. Box 8000 • Tyler, TX 75711